THE MYTH OF LIVING THE CHRISTIAN LIFE

REALLY ENJOYING THE CHRISTIAN LIFE
INSTEAD OF JUST ENDURING IT

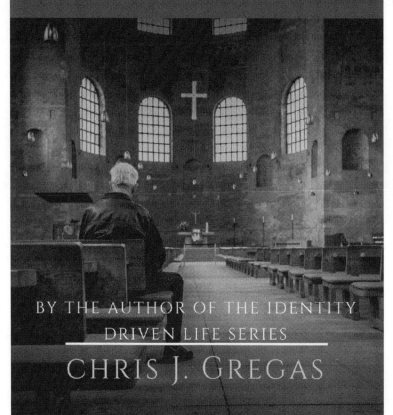

BY THE AUTHOR OF THE IDENTITY
DRIVEN LIFE SERIES

CHRIS J. GREGAS

Introduction

This book is dedicated to all those gifted teachers of the New Testament who have made clarity and the complete story of the Christian life their aim. Among these are Dr. Neil Anderson, Watchman Nee, Charles Solomon, Hudson Taylor, Miles Stanford and the apostle Paul. I am forever indebted to your faithfulness to the Lord and your passion to walk in a manner worthy of your calling.

It has been my desire almost from the inception of my Christian walk to set the record straight as to what this life and walk entails. I have been ever growing through the years in my understanding of how to let Christ, who is my life, direct this life and heart of mine. It has been agonizing and exhilarating all at the same time.

It is my hope as I set this book in front of you that you find the same challenge and encouragement that I had it writing it and as I have allowed Christ to live it in and through me through the years. Satan does not want you to read this book. I can pretty much guarantee as much. He does not want you to come to grips with the biblical mandate of Christ as it relates to Christian living. He would just as soon see you continue to grind it out and stress over your life until you are finally released into eternity.

This book will allow you to see the Christian life in most of its fulness. Not all of it because of my limited knowledge here on earth and because the best of this life – is yet to come. Yet, we must know how to live and who is living this life if we are ever to please God and make Him famous. To this end, I labor and write so that Jesus may be praised, and Christians built up in the most holy faith.

In Christ, Chris J. Gregas

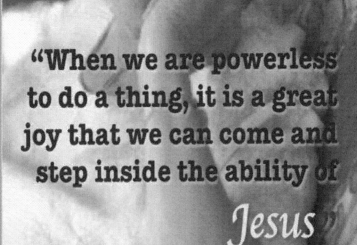

"When we are powerless
to do a thing, it is a great
joy that we can come and
step inside the ability of

Jesus"

-Corrie ten Boom

Corrie ten Boom Museum

Table of Contents

1

The Myth of Living the Christian Life

"God is most glorified in us when we are most satisfied in Him" -John Piper

"People create the sort of myths they want to believe about themselves." -Clint Smith

Myth :

a traditional story, especially one concerning the early history of a people or explaining some natural or social phenomenon, and typically involving supernatural beings or events. A widely held but false belief or idea.

What do you believe about life that is worth talking about and passing along to others? Is your world/life view full of confidence or does it have a bit of mystery and doubt peppered in? How you answer will determine whether you wish to leave a spiritual legacy where it matters.

One of the most mythical and mysterious creatures of North America and Canada is the hairy man-beast known as the *"Sasquatch or better known as Bigfoot."* Supposedly a throwback to our evolutionary past, it is an "ape-man" version of us as humans. What most people don't know is that the first reported sighting of such a creature dates back until the early 1800's. For over two hundred years this legend and mythical figure has fascinated the masses and at the same time made a fair group of men and women spend years of their life trying to prove Bigfoot's existence.

Whether you believe Bigfoot is real or a mythical figure that has been type casted, this creature fits the bill of what we call a *"myth."* Myths are quite powerful in almost any form and they have the ability to lead people to a place where they never thought they would travel to. This is also true in the spiritual realm. Men and women seeking the truth but turning to myths and rote tradition can be almost a worse case of being led astray than any mythical creature ever could.

I have a simple question as we begin this literary journey together.

What would you give or sacrifice to have inner peace and joy on an ongoing basis?

I am not ashamed to say that I have fallen out of the sky hundreds of times in attempting to live out the Christian life. Maybe you can relate. Maybe you, like me, are or have been, sick and tired of being sick and tired and are more than ready for – *real, definitive change.*

I have some further questions for you to think over as we take this journey together.

How would you define the Christian life?

Why didn't God save you and then immediately transport you to Heaven that very hour He delivered you?

Does it matter to you how you walk and live in this world and does it matter to you that there might be a biblical blueprint that makes the journey a whole lot less dramatic?

What would you give or do to bring a smile to God's face on a consistent basis? And do you think that is possible?

These questions and many more will be thoroughly investigated in this book. There is no way for you to read this book and not see the direction of your mind and heart begin to long for more - more of Jesus and what He gracefully dispenses. That is my prayer for you and for all the others who will (along the way) also take this trip with us.

Now, it is certainly no secret that there is a boatload of ideas that we grew up believing that are, in fact, **totally false.** Old wife's tales and epic legend are powerful things in this world and in the world of thought. Let me give you a just few of these *"myths"* you undoubtedly grew up with. (**Disclaimer**: *These* **myths** *have all been debunked so I will give no further explanation.*)

- *You should wash your chicken before you cook it.*
- *You actually lose most of your body heat through your head.*
- *Watching TV too close to the screen will not make you go blind.*
- *Brown eggs are better and more nutritious than white eggs.*
- *Left-brained people are more logical and right-brained people are more creative.*
- *Don't eat and swim, you will drown.*
- *Never touch baby birds.*
- *We only use ten percent of our brain.*
- *Bats are blind.*
- *Toads cause you to get warts.*
- *A broken mirror gives you seven years of bad luck.*

And the list goes on and on. I think you get the picture. Myths and false reports are what makes the world go around and unfortunately, they make, to a point, *the Christian church go around as well.*

Much of the Newer Testament centers around evil static in the line and consistent drama concerning the ministry of false teachers. Those who peddle lies and myths, hoping to capture and enslave unsuspecting and illiterate believers. At the end of the day, we become the sum of what we believe and what we are willing to trust in. And if what we believe is not rooted in **truth**, we will be on a fast track that yields *spiritual and emotional upheaval.*

The great writer G.K. Chesterton once observed that the Christian ideal has not been tried and found wanting. It has been found difficult and left untried. I must agree with him.

There is a debilitating myth when it comes to living the Christian life that has the Christian church worldwide by the scruff of the neck. It has not always been this way, but it certainly is the culture that affects the church presently. It is **man centered** in nature and it is **works centered** in its explanation and application. It is a scandal across the church that is long overdue in giving this the urgent attention it deserves.

It is my goal throughout this book and in this chapter to *explode* the prevailing myths that are spoiling the wonderful truths that center in on living for Jesus Christ. *What does that mean and how do we get back to the Newer Testament pattern of Christian living?* By God's grace, I will hammer this question out.

The *Myth* Of Living The Christian Life

I want to, for the remainder of this first chapter, explode and uncover **"myths"** that permeate throughout the Christian church concerning - Christian living. These are some of the most common myths and beliefs of what it means to live out the Christian life and walk. The Russian leader Lenin once said, *"Give me four years to teach the children and the seed I have sown will never be uprooted."* Take the time and read this book and you can never be the same again. I will only touch on these briefly on what the Newer Testament teaches about the Christian life and the logic behind it. I will also, in later chapters, put skin on the bones in this area. You ready? Here we go. Strap on your headphones – and your helmet.

Christian Life Myth #1 *"Living the Christian life is solely or mostly -* ***up to us.****"*

In other words, living the Christian life squares mostly on the believer's shoulders. In this belief, Christ is more of a *helper* and it is on *us (the helped)* to live out the Christian life. This myth seems to be the most prolific of beliefs across Christianity. In fact, I am sure that most of you who are reading this have either been exposed to this reasoning or are actually living by this belief. Yet, I want you to think about what it means when we call it a *"Christian life."*

Notice, it is not a "believers' life or a Christian's life", but a Christian life which means that Christ is or must be the motivator and main driver of such a life. Christ being a Divine helper in the process just doesn't explain adequately what in fact the Newer Testament says about this life. And it is a myth and a grave mistake to believe that the Christian life is mostly or solely up to us or attained through our own increased strength and/or effort.

Christian Life Myth #2 *"Living the Christian life hoping to improve as a Christian."*

I have heard people say concerning the Christian life, *"this room for improvement is the largest room in the world."* But the question is, *how do we improve on a life that is essentially not ours?* We must come to realize (*and we will discuss this in detail by book's end*) that the most important part of Christian is the – *first six letters!* Think about this. Since we have a new nature that is perfect (2 Peter 1:4) this certainly cannot nor does not need to be improved upon. How can you and I improve upon perfect and divine? And since Romans 6:6 tells us that our old nature (self) was, once for all, crucified with Christ, we cannot nor do we have to improve upon that which is already dead as a doornail. *Improving ourselves* in the Christian life is not only a myth but it is totally illogical when we understand what took place when we were given by grace - new life in Christ.

Christian Life Myth #3 *"The Christian life cannot be enjoyed so it is be endured."*

"Years in the ministry have taught me that many people *endure* the Christian life rather than *enjoy* it." So, says, Christian leader and Pastor, Stephen Olford, in his book,

Not I, But Christ. I maintain that more than some believers have bought into the erroneous idea that the Christian life is just not what it's cracked up to be. So, they must "gut it out" until they die, or when Jesus comes to deliver them from their tortured state. In this realm, the Christian experience becomes more of a *chore* than a *celebration*. It is more endured than enjoyed, The only problem with this, is that this doesn't even sound remotely close to what Jesus said when He walked this earth. (i.e. John 10:10) We were made for so much more. Those who are caught in this web of deceit are active for a while but usually become casualties in the Christian life and church and it is all because their understanding of the Christian life is based on a – myth.

Christian Life Myth #4 *"The Christian life is really **hard work** and a **constant struggle** to succeed and advance."*

Most Christians would say that living for Christ takes hard work, constant work and continued effort. That sounds right and it even sounds real, but is it true that is the question? There is no denying that millions of believers in Christ are working their full heads off in their attempt to successfully succeed in their Christian walk. As I alluded to before, there are to many as well who are now on the sideline because they could not keep up the pace of what they and others expected of them along the way. They have resigned themselves to doing *"the best they can"* and hope for the best when they get to Heaven. *But is that what Christ expects of us? Is that what the Good Shepherd gave His life for the sheep for?* We are certainly told in scripture to *"work out our salvation"* and that we are saved "to good works", but what does that mean exactly? Is hard work and effort coupled with intense struggle the means we live the

Christian life successfully. Not if we understand what the Christian life truly is. Stay tuned. I will develop this in more detail as the chapters roll out.

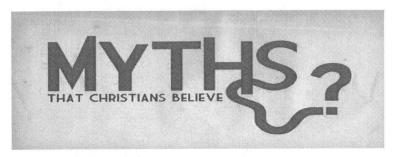

Christian Life Myth #5 *"The Christian life is all about - letting go and letting God."*

This seems to be highly celebrated by those who seem to understand *to a point* what the Newer Testament says about the Christian life. But in this myth, they travel a bridge to far with an imbalanced view of how the Christian life works. To say that the Trinity is totally responsible for our Christian life is never the message of scripture. Nor does it say that it is all on us or up to us.

Mike Jantzen, in an article entitled, **6 Myths About the Abundant Life**, writes these words, *"Some Christians expect God to somehow hand them an abundant Christian life with minimal risk-taking, soul-searching, or work on their part.*

We are not entitled to abundance. Life to the full comes through obedience accomplished in the Spirit's strength. The greatest parts of the Christian life come through gaining victory in spiritual battles: fending off temptation, learning to put others first, letting go of our plans, remaining available to God no matter the cost.

Grace does not exclude work; it empowers it. It teaches us to say "No" to ungodliness and worldly passions, and to live self-controlled, upright and godly lives in this present age (Titus 2:12).

So, let's run to God, hold on to him, and commit to doing whatever he asks in his power.

Let's take up St. Augustine's motto, "All abundance, which is not my God, is emptiness to me" (The Confessions).

Then we will no longer be infants, tossed back and forth by the waves, and blown here and there by every wind of teaching [...] Instead, speaking the truth in love, we will grow to become in every respect the mature body of him who is the head, that is, Christ (Ephesians 4:14-15).

Our lives will become abundantly full of meaning, joy, love, and purpose as we learn to walk more and more constantly under the direction of the Spirit, trusting him for the power to obey."

The truth of the matter is, there is a clear divine partnership that makes the Christian life work, and we will look at this in real detail in the next chapter. This myth might sound liberating but without a proper balance, it is eventually a turn off to both the one who is knee deep in it and to those who are down wind from it.

Christian Life Myth #6 *"We are just **a sinner saved by grace** and therefore we must do the best we can to live for Christ."*

This myth, in this writer's humble opinion, is embedded deeply in the Christian church. You might say, *what is wrong with this statement and how is this a – myth?* Well, think about this. While it is true, that we were (*in our unredeemed state*) a sinner that was saved purely by the grace and mercy of Christ, that is not who we are **now** as children of the living God. The Bible, specifically, the Newer Testament, calls God's children **saints,** not **sinners.** We are **now** *(in our saved state)* saints who sometimes sin and when God looks at us, He sees us fully robed in the righteousness of Christ. (2 Corinthians 5:21) The question is, are we going to continue to be **sin-conscious** or **saint-conscious?** Are we going to continue to try harder so we can feel good about ourselves and our walk or are we going to enjoy who we are *in Christ* now that He has rescued us from the kingdom of darkness? Remember: We become in attitude and action what we actually – believe. (Prov. 23:7)

Christian Life Myth #7 *"God truly helps those who **help themselves.***"

It is amazing to know that so many religious people believe this statement is in the Bible. It is not. Although he didn't invent it, Benjamin Franklin is generally held to have popularized this motto in his *Poor Richard's Almanac.* Probably not a good idea to fashion your Christian life after old Ben. So, its stands to reason that if we can't trust in ourselves, then what hope do we have in Christian living? Fortunately, the Bible has an answer. The prophet Isaiah declares that ***God helps those who are utterly helpless.*** (Isaiah 25:4) God provides powerfully for those who are *helpless* and *needy*. We might say it this way. God helps those who ***can't*** help themselves. The person who tries to help himself or herself is going to be spiritually defeated on a regular basis. And in our Christian walk, we must realize as soon as possible that without

Christ, *we can do nothing of eternal value.* (John 15:4-5) That means exactly what it says. This myth is dead on arrival and it should be.

Question: How many of these "myths" have you bought in to? How many have you come to believe are a major part of your Christian life? Are you interested in finding out what is left when it comes to – how we live the Christian life? You are in for a real treat and your life can never be the same. That ought to whet your appetite unless you are void of a pulse.

The Results of Believing Myths and Lies?

Believing lies and popular myths have their own devastating results, and none can be more harmful to the soul than being misinformed about how to live the life that has been given to us at a great cost by Christ. When you think seriously about this, *is there anything sadder than this?*

First, **believing myths and lies choke out the truth in our lives.** Unfortunately, we cannot buy into lies and still stand strong on the truth. It is like being filled with darkness and expecting to be a shining example of light. It cannot happen. If we are ever to find the truth of God for our freedom (i.e., John 8:31-36) we must reject the myths and hold dearly to the truth even if it is somewhat foreign to our thinking. Someone wisely said, *"People don't set out to build their faith on myths. Yet many myths and falsehoods have been handed down from generation to generation that shape the way a lot of Christians think about life and God. These beliefs are assumed by many to be rock-solid truth - until life proves they are not. The tragic result is often a* *spiritual disaster - confusion, feelings of betrayal, distrust of Scripture, and a loss of faith or anger toward both God and church."*

Second, ***myths and lies have their origin in the devil himself.*** Jesus said that plainly in John 8:44. *Is it any Christian's desire "deep down" to follow the enemy of their souls with a carefree and happy attitude?* Not over the long haul. Why would we want to legitimize and support what Satan and his minions are doing? The reason why we must be sober minded when it comes to lies and myths is because of ***who*** is propagating them. A carefree attitude in this regard is to be deceived at the highest level and that is never good for the child of God.

Lastly, ***to not understand (or to misunderstand) how to live the Christian life is at the very root of you living ineffectively and God getting great glory from your life.*** Think about how depressing it is for someone or something to not thrive or function as to their calling and ability? When a car begins to have internal problems, we know that this was not the original makeup and plan for it. When a body goes south and disease seem to take over, we are all aware that the body itself is not functioning in a healthy and balanced manner. And when the child of God is ignorant or ill-prepared to live out the life that God has deposited in us, then we are out of kilter and unable to become what we have been reborn to become. And that is the gravest epitaph of all for any of us.

This first chapter is in the books. We are just getting started and the next chapter is really going to begin a wildfire in you about the joy and peace that Christ is more than willing to provide to you in your Christian walk and life. Let's go!

2

Is It Either Or / Or Both And?

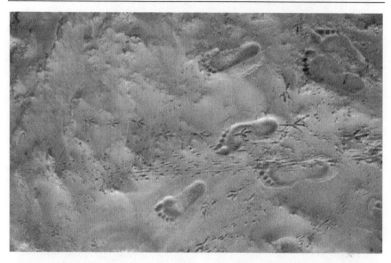

"For we are laborers together with God: You are God's vineyard; you are God's building" (1 Corinthians 3:9)

"The life of the believer is not in himself, but in his Lord: "He that has the Son has life; and he that has not the Son of God has not life." "I live," says the apostle Paul; "yet not I, but Christ lives in me;" and, writing to the Colossians, he says, "For you are dead, and your life is hidden with Christ in God." Just as this finger of mine lives because of its union with the head, and with the heart, and with the rest of my being where life is to be found, so do you and I live because we have been joined unto Christ. If there were no life in the stem, there would be no life in the branch. If the branch is severed from the vine, it has no life in itself." -C.H. Spurgeon

Once the devil was walking along with one of his demons. They saw a man ahead of them pick up something shiny. "What did he just pick up?" asked the demon. "A piece of the truth," the devil replied. "Doesn't it bother you that he found a piece of the truth?" asked the demon. "No," said the devil, "I will see to it that he makes a religion out of it." *(Klyne Snodgrass, Between Two Truths - Living with Biblical Tensions, 1990, Zondervan Publishing House, p. 35.)*

The moral of the story? *Satan and mankind find it rather easy to twist the truth enough to shade its true meaning.*

I learned a while back that - *life is all about balance.* It is all about partnership.

Sam Metcalf tells this story about the need for balance in every area of our lives. *"I remember playing a game as a child in which we would bend one knee and grab our foot behind us and then try to race—limping, stumbling and falling over as we struggled across the grass toward a finish line. That is what happens when we have only one leg to stand on or assume that somehow two left feet suffice for one of each. This balancing act is repeated throughout most of nature. Two eyes to give perspective. Two arms and two hands to provide dexterity. Two sides of our brain that tandem. All these things come in pairs because there are many things in the physical world that work best when they have balance and complementarity."*

If you ever see a turtle high on a fence post, you will have to conclude that he had help to get there. *The Christian life is all about partnership and balance as well.* If we don't understand that and do not fully buy into this classic Bible

teaching, then we will struggle and be defeated our whole Christian life. *Is that what you want? I thought so.*
So, when we look at the partnership that we have entered into with Christ when he redeemed us, the all-important question is:

Whose **responsibility** *is it to act in the Christian life:* **Christ or ours?** Great question. The answer is coming to a theater near you.

Let me briefly share a little of my own personal story. When I first came to know Christ, (or better yet to be known by Him) I did what all new believers tend to do - *I went from one extreme to the other* – on a regular basis – without knowing what kind of rollercoaster I was really on. I had no earthly idea how to live this new life and worse yet, I largely got in the way of the One [Christ] who said He would live it in me and more importantly - *through me.*

I had a college professor that was a broken record when it came to reminding us that life is all about – *balance.* The challenge to find balance in our Christian walk is one of the biggest challenges of our lives. We, at the start, do not know how to balance the need to *walk* and be active and the art of – *waiting on God.* That is the balance beam we must walk on as we move closer toward our heavenly home.

Jesus is and was amazing for so many reasons. His no nonsense approach to life left a sweet aroma along the countryside of Israel but it also cut to pieces those who were addicted and at home with spiritual darkness. I am completely ruined by the eye-opening statement Jesus made to the crowds (*and of course His followers*) one day in the Judean desert. Can *you* imagine hearing these barn burning words yourself?

"Come to me, all of you who are weary and burdened, and I will give you rest. Take up my yoke and learn from me, because I am lowly and humble in heart, and you will find rest for your souls. For my yoke is easy and my burden is light." (Matthew 11:28-30 – CSB)

Wow. Now that is a mouthful. As we develop this chapter, I want to spend a few moments talking about *how important* Jesus is to our Christian life. After all, He is the author and finisher of our faith. (Heb. 12:2) In the end, my prayer is that you and I will be motivated to echo what Peter said when he told the Lord that - *we (I, him, us) can go to no other who has the words of eternal life than our Lord.* But we must be convinced of that.

I want you to notice that first Jesus says **come to *Me***. He did not strong arm them to a cause or a popular fad or even some famous guru of the day. He says I am the One who can meet your needs. I am the One who you need to come to and look to. Come to me though you might hesitate. Do not look anywhere else. The answer to your desperate search for "real life" is *Me* and the end of your search is at *My* provision and direction.

Then He says, all those who tired and weighed down emotionally and spiritually – **come to *Me***.

In other words, do not put your trust in your doctor or your medications or your strong man or woman. If you are sick and tired of being sick and tired and you are burdened to the max, you know who to come to. I am here in plain sight. I am not far away. It may seem that way, but nothing could be further from the truth. Satan is a liar. I am He who you have been looking for your whole life.

Then He gives a sweeping offer and promise to all those who **come to Him** because they have bottomed out. *"I will give you rest and inner peace."*

Now there's an offer that will get anybody who is listening - attention. We have all tried to find inner rest through a myriad of ways and means. While some things seem to give temporary relief, nothing in this fallen world - seems to fit forever. Pleasures and experiences quiet the noise for a moment but the real peace that all of us are on the search for is elusive at best. Yet, the promise of Jesus is simple and to the point. **Come to Me** and I will give you what you have been searching for through many long winters. We would be a real fool to not at least investigate His offer. Our burdened souls only truly find rest in one place: *"For God alone, O my soul, wait in silence, for my hope is from him. He only is my rock and my salvation, my fortress; I shall not be shaken. On God rests my salvation and my glory; my mighty rock, my refuge is God."* (**Psalm 62:5-7**)

Then He offers a *challenge.* This challenge is certainly not for the fainthearted. *"Take my yoke on you."*

Say what Jesus? What does that mean? Jesus was saying that you (we) need to welcome His teaching over and above the teaching of the world and its teachers. You and I need to accept His way and not the way of the culture. It is so easy to bypass Christ for what we are comfortable with or dialed into, but the real deal is in the way and university of Christ. The Master Teacher of every generation.

Come to *Me* and buy into my teaching and way. *"Learn from Me"* he adds. It is certainly not wrong to learn from others, but Jesus says let it be chiefly from – *Me* and let your teachers be mostly from Me. Come to my school and learn what real, eternal learning looks like. Learn from Me and you will never lack for understanding, especially when it comes to the deep things of God. Wow! What an offer and challenge.

Then Jesus tells the crowd (and His followers) *why* they should come to Him and learn from Him. Simply because - *I (Jesus) am humble enough to teach you and submissive enough to my Father for Him to lead you as He leads Me.*

There it is in plain view. The divinely infused character of the Father was the strength of his conduct and authoritative teaching. So, it is with us. The Christian life and walk are all about *His character* sweetly wrought in and through us so that *our conduct* might flow from His blessed inner work. Praise His great Name! *Can it get any better than this?*

Again, He promises inner rest and joy simply because we come to Him. The One who is divinely humble, when we in turn humble ourselves to become the instrument of the Divine, what a recipe for good and godliness is cooked up in our lives. And the beat goes on.

Well, our Savior closes this landmark homily with the simple but sweeping statement, *"For my yoke is easy and my burden is light."*

I personally believe He set the crowd up for that statement. It was all predicated on the profound words - **Come to *Me*** – period without pause or hesitation.

Why?

Because you are emotionally and spiritually tired and overly burdened.

Because He is the One who can truly give you real and lasting spiritual rest and inner peace.

Because you can learn from someone who is totally humble and perfectly submissive to the Father - and what a lesson that might be.

Because my teaching and way of life is much more freeing than anything the world offers or educates you with.

A Prayer for the Weary to Find Rest

Father, I come to you and your Son and ask for your rest and peace. I pray you lift this burden of doing and striving off of my shoulders and take away my desire to work to exhaustion. Allow me to sit in Your presence and let You do all of the spiritual work. I pray you mold me into Your image, instilling in me a restful spirit. Let me radiate Your peace onto others, even in the midst of chaos, and show me how to walk down the path of rest that has at the end You. In Jesus Name - Amen.

So. As we investigate who is responsible for our Christian life, we know one thing for sure. Jesus is all we need, and in the end - all we got. He is the One who you and I have been looking for your whole life and He is the One who is able to keep you from falling and to present you faultless before His throne.

With that in mind, for the remainder of the chapter, let's discuss the *"substance"* of what it means to live a life that is Christian. Let us balance the books as to who and what this Christian walk looks like, really looks like or at the very least – *should look like*.

John Piper asks these important questions, *"How do you go about living the Christian life in such a way that you are actually doing the living, doing the acting, and doing the willing, and yet Christ, or the Holy Spirit, is decisively doing the living, and doing the acting, and doing the willing in and through your acting, willing, and doing? How do I work hard and yet be able to say when I am done, 'God's grace was the worker in and through me'?"* That is the key issue, it seems to me, of the Christian life. That's the way Paul says he lived. And he means for us to live that way. He says in 1 Corinthians 15:10, *"By the grace of God I am what I am, and his grace toward me was not in vain. On the contrary, I worked harder than any of them, though it was not I, but the grace of God that is with me." (How Do I Live an Authentic Christian Life, John Piper Message, February 22, 2016)*

How do we "reconcile the two" as believers in Christ?
Let's talk about it because it is extremely important that we understand this. If not, we are going to continue to spin our wheels as a Church and personally and the devil will make a spiritual killing all the way to the bank. It seems to me that much of the confusion concerning the Christian life and walk have been the *two extremes* that seem to motor this confusion and chaos.

On the one hand, we have Christian leaders and the sheep who believe that it is *all of Christ* performing the work and that we need to *"let go and let God"* and sit and wait for the heavenly paycheck to come to the mailbox. It is a clear passive view of the Christian life and it seems to celebrate waiting rather than work and welfare rather than activity.

On the other side of the spectrum, the Christian church teaches a philosophy that essentially says, ***"if it's gonna be, it's up to me."*** In this model, we are the engine that makes this Christian walk – ride like the wind or flame out. It is more man-sided in its approach. Certainly, Christ is a main cog in the wheel, but He is more like a helper and assister than the actual ball of wax.

Let's go back to my original question. ***Is it either or – or both and as it relates to the Christian life?*** Who is responsible for living the Christian life? I think by now you know the answer, according to the scriptures. Let's unpack this *"both and..."* path for living out the Christian life for the remainder of the chapter. It will be a rich study indeed.

Either Or / Or Both And?

Either/Or Approach. This approach to Christian living, is in this writer's opinion, *never supported by or in scripture.* Now there is clearly a divine and clear **partnership** in living out the Christian life. The problem historically has been that Christian churches have not always been balanced in this area. That is always one of the problems with how we live. A ***life of imbalance*** (*as I said before*) seems to curse us and stop our growth at every turn. We swing one way or the other without too much concern about landing in the middle. But the middle, balanced, is where we need to be – sooner rather than later. God's glory in and through us *is at stake,* when you get right down to it.

It is no secret that - *The Christian life is a spiritual battle which the Bible exhorts us to prepare for and wage war diligently.* "Fight the good fight of faith" (1 Timothy 6:12); "Endure hardship . . . like a good soldier of Christ Jesus" (2 Timothy 2:3); "Put on the full armor of God so that you can take your stand against the devil's schemes" (Ephesians 6:11). Letting go and letting God do it all for us, and sitting back and watching events unfold, however they may unfold, is not biblical or even wise.

Having said that, though, we must understand that the things we are to do as a Christian, we do by the power of God and not in our own steam. We must remember that God will never do for us what, we must do ourselves. But we also must be assured of this: *We can never do or pull off what only God can do.* Don't miss that.

So, in the Christian life what exactly are we to do and what does God take responsibility for?

Both/And Approach. On the other hand, the **"both/and approach"** can heartily be supported by scripture. That is, *the Christian life is 100% Christ and 100% - us.* You say, "Chris, where do you come to that conclusion?" Listen to what the apostle Paul says to the Philippian believers.

Therefore, my beloved, as you have always obeyed, so now, not only as in my presence but much more in my absence, work out your own salvation with fear and trembling, for it is God who works in you, both to will and to work for his good pleasure. **(Phil. 2:12-13)**

There is no way to look at these verses without concluding that there is a *"divine partnership"* that Christ and us - *must enter into together.* The Christian life does not work without both of us doing what we are responsible for.

It is identical to a marriage. How so you may ask?

Just for the record, I myself married a very capable and hardworking woman. When we got married, I had a lazy streak running through me due to not having a lot of confidence in work itself and also because I knew that I could not keep up with the energizer bunny I married so why try? So, for the first decade of our marriage, it was almost a "one man [*in my case one woman*] show" and it was not good. We had a good marriage but the underlying *"fly in the ointment"* was that I just refused to carry my weight around the house and pitch in. It nearly cost us our marriage. I falsely believed that since my wife was so capable and able to leap a tall building in a single bound, I did not need to seriously enter in a partnership with her when it came to the important work of the home, including helping with the young and energetic children.

The Christian life can never work powerfully without us having a proper marriage (partnership) with our Groomsman, Jesus Christ. Since we are His bride, we must know that He is rooting for us to succeed and He is ever desirous for us to be in perfect precision with His work around the world. But that will never happen if we fail to realize what Christ's work is and what ours is. What we are responsible for and what only He can pull off by His omnipotent hand.

Partnership with God is vital in anything we do in this life as His children. Robert Pace reminds us of this, *"God*

~ 29 ~

desires to partner with people so they can manifest His purposes in the earth. And the Bible says this is possible if we would seek to "know Him." Daniel 11:32 says: "the people who know their God will be strong and do exploits." The NAS version puts it this way: It says the people that know their God would "display strength and take action." This means a special relationship with God is available if we will seek to claim it!

Look at men of Scripture that lived in partnership with God:

Noah's partnership with God saved his family from the Flood and preserved humanity.

Abraham's partnership with God also made a global impact. His faith secured the Promised Land for the Hebrew people and brought spiritual blessings to every nation.

Jacob's partnership with God brought him multiplied wealth even while laboring with his conniving father-in-law.

Moses experienced "face to face" fellowship with God (Deut. 34:10). And he liberated two million Jews from Egypt!

And Joshua secured a military alliance with God that conquered the Canaanites and settled the Hebrew tribes in the Promised Land. Joshua's partnership with God was so phenomenal, that without earthly assistance, the angels flattened Jericho's impregnable walls!

Wouldn't you like to live this way? Wouldn't you like to claim such a close posture with God that he dispatched angels to work in your behalf?

Well, it is possible! You can claim partnership with God in a unique and powerful way! This is what I want to discuss in my first point. Partnership with God begins by discerning your spiritual birthright." (Source: https://revelationcentral.com/partnership-with-god/)

There is an old saying that says, *"God gives the birds their food, but He doesn't throw it into their nests."* That makes perfect sense when we look at the Christian life. His work in and through us is done by His power mightily working in us. Our work is a **work of faith** that trusts in Jesus to do in us and through us what can only be pulled off by the Divine. A true partnership made in Heaven and maintained and carried out on earth and in time. Now that is the kind of relationship that pays dividends not only here but in eternity. Praise His Great Name!

3

A Changed Life or An Exchanged Life?

"We think of the Christian life as a 'changed life' but it is not that. What God offers us is an 'exchanged life,' a 'substituted life,' and Christ is our substitute within." -Watchman Nee, The Normal Christian Life

When Christ calls a man, He bids him to come and die." –Dietrich Bonhoeffer

The great Bible professor, Howard Hendricks once said that there are – *"Three stages people go through when confronted with change: Resistance to change, Tolerant of change and the embracing of change."* (**Howard Hendricks, in The Monday Morning Mission**.)

With the first two stages in place and without the last, *(embracing of change)* a man or woman can never accept and capitalize on the prevailing winds and benefit of real change. I don't want to be *"that guy or girl."* I hope you feel the same way.

In this chapter, we are not only going to see the kind of change that happened at our spiritual conversion, but we also are going to be challenged to the max as to how we might change our thinking to what we have thought in the past. You will understand what I am getting to as we develop this chapter.

Whenever we talk about the Christian life, we must talk about *what happened* when we became a true Christian. *What actually took place? What changed about us if anything? What spiritual position do we now enjoy as a child of God? What abilities and availability (if any) have we been given to live for Christ so we can please Him in this walk of faith we have started?* I think you would agree these are all important questions that we must answer.

We all must come to the realization that - ***experiencing the new birth is a divine miracle.*** Jesus described it as being born again, born anew or born of the Spirit. Put another way, born a second time, this time spiritually and not merely physically. It is a change of identity and destiny, but it is also a new life that does not boast in outward reformation but divinely inward transformation. Jesus went on to say (*recorded in John chapter 3*) **that unless a man or woman is born again,** they cannot see or get to the kingdom of God which in biblical terms is – **Heaven.** That is how important it is to be born anew. Without it, there is **no knowing** about Heaven. Without it, there is no **going to** Heaven. That makes it an all-encompassing matter than cannot be overlooked or ignored. To do so would be the greatest of mistakes.

In this chapter, we want to build on what we started. I want to look at the idea of being changed when we come to be known by Christ. And is it really a *change* or an *exchange*? You might say, *"what do you mean Chris by – an exchange?"* I want to develop a ghostly truth today that has been effectively phased out of church teaching altogether, and we wonder why so many of God's people are defeated and hanging on by a thread spiritually speaking.

A Heartfelt Letter That Says It All

In order to get this matter started, I want to share with you a letter from a missionary to China named **J. Hudson Taylor**. His ministry throughout the inland area of China nearly 150 years ago, helped pave the way for such a vibrant evangelical movement throughout all of China today. He was a powerful instrument in the hand of Christ there, *but it was not always so.* The truth is Taylor's Christian walk and spiritual life was seriously on the ropes shortly after he began to minister in China. The following letter is to his sister Amelia, written in 1869. It is a little lengthy but I give it to you in its entirety because the flavor of it drives home what I want to communicate in this chapter. It is a letter of rejoicing over what Christ can do in a life that understands their secure union with Him. ***Read it to the end or you will miss its full impact*** and see if you can at all relate to this young missionary's battle. In this letter we see the Christian life and struggle in all its beauty.

 *My own dear Sister -*

"So many thanks for your long, dear letter... I do not think you have written me such a letter since we have been in China. I know it is with you as with me—you cannot, not you will not. Mind and body will not bear more than a certain amount of strain or do more than a certain amount of work. As to work, mine was never so plentiful, so

responsible, or so difficult; but the weight and strain are all gone. The last month or more has been perhaps, the happiest of my life; and I long to tell you a little of what the Lord has done for my soul. I do not know how far I may be able to make myself intelligible about it, for there is nothing new or strange or wonderful—and yet, all is new! In a word, "Whereas once I was blind, now I see."

Perhaps I shall make myself clearer if I go back a little. Well, dearie, my mind has been greatly exercised for six or eight months past, feeling the need personally, and for our Mission, of more holiness, life, power in our souls. But personal need stood first and was the greatest. I felt the ingratitude, the danger, the sin of not living nearer to God. I prayed, agonized, fasted, strove, made resolutions, read the Word more diligently, sought more time for retirement and meditation—but all was without effect. Every day, almost every hour, the consciousness of sin oppressed me. I knew that if I could only abide in Christ all would be well, but I could not. I began the day with prayer, determined not to take my eye from Him for a moment; but pressure of duties, sometimes very trying, constant interruptions apt to be so wearing, often caused me to forget Him. Then one's nerves get so fretted in this climate that temptations to irritability, hard thoughts, and sometimes unkind words are all the more difficult to control. Each day brought its register of sin and failure, of lack of power. To will was indeed present with me, but how to perform I found not.

Then came the question, "Is there no rescue? Must it be thus, to the end—constant conflict and, instead of victory, too often defeat?" How, too, could I preach with sincerity that to those who receive Jesus, "to them gave the power to become the sons of God" (i.e. God-like) when it was not so in my own experience? Instead of growing stronger, I seemed to be getting weaker and to have less power against sin; and no wonder, for faith and even hope was getting very low. I hated myself; I hated my sin; and yet I gained no strength against it. I felt I was a child of God: His Spirit in my heart would cry, in spite of all, "Abba, Father": but to rise to my privileges as a child, I was utterly powerless.

I thought that holiness, practical holiness, was to be gradually attained by a diligent use of the means of grace. I felt that there was nothing I so much desired in this world, nothing I so much needed. But so far from in any measure attaining it, the more I pursued and strove after it, the more it eluded my grasp; till hope itself almost died out, and I began to think that, perhaps to make heaven the sweeter, God would not give it down here. I do not think I was striving to attain it in my own strength. I knew I was powerless. I told the Lord so and asked Him to give me help and strength; and sometimes I almost believed He would keep and uphold me. But on looking back in the evening, alas! there was but sin and failure to confess and mourn before God.

I would not give you the impression that this was the daily experience of all those long, weary months. It was a too frequent state of soul; that toward which I was tending, and which almost ended in despair. And yet never did Christ seem more precious—a Savior who could and would save such a sinner! ... And sometimes there were seasons not only of peace but of joy in the Lord. But they were transitory, and at best there was a sad lack of power. Oh, how good the Lord was in bringing this conflict to an end!

All the time I felt assured that there was in Christ all I needed, but the practical question was how to get it out. He was rich, truly, but I was poor; He strong, but I weak. I knew full well that there was in the root, the stem, abundant fatness; but how to get it into my puny little branch was the question. As gradually the light was dawning on me, I saw that faith was the only prerequisite, was the hand to lay hold on His fulness and make it my own. But I had not this faith. I strove for it, but it would not come; tried to exercise it, but in vain. Seeing more and more the wondrous supply of grace laid up in Jesus, the fulness of our precious Savior—my helplessness and guilt seemed to increase. Sins committed appeared but as trifles compared with the sin of unbelief, which was their cause, which could not or would not take God at His word, but rather made Him a liar! Unbelief was, I felt, the damning sin of the world—yet I indulged in it. I prayed for faith, but it came not. What was I to do?

When my agony of soul was at its height, a sentence in a letter from dear McCarthy [John McCarthy, in Hangchow] was used to remove the scales from my eyes, and the Spirit of God revealed the truth of our oneness with Jesus as I had never known it before. McCarthy, who had been much exercised by the same sense of failure, but saw the light before I did, wrote (I quote from memory):

"But how to get faith strengthened? Not by striving after faith, but by resting on the Faithful One."

As I read, I saw it all! "If we believe not, He abides faithful." I looked to Jesus and saw (and when I saw, oh, how joy flowed!) that He had said, "I will never leave you." "Ah, there is rest!" I thought. "I have striven in vain to rest in Him. I'll strive no more. For has He not promised to abide with me—never to leave me, never to fail me?" And, dearie, He never will!

But this was not all He showed me, nor one half. As I thought of the Vine and the branches, what light the blessed Spirit poured direct into my soul! How great seemed my mistake in having wished to get the sap, the fulness out of Him. I saw not only that Jesus would never leave me, but that I was a member of His body, of His flesh and of His bones. The vine now I see, is not the root merely, but all— root, stem, branches, twigs, leaves, flowers, fruit: and Jesus is not only that: He is soil and sunshine, air and showers, and ten thousand times more than we have ever dreamed, wished for, or needed. Oh, the joy of seeing this truth! I do pray that the eyes of your understanding may be enlightened, that you may know and enjoy the riches freely given us in Christ.

Oh, my dear sister, it is a wonderful thing to be really one with a risen and exalted Savior; to be a member of Christ! Think what it involves. Can Christ be rich and I poor? Can your right hand be rich and the left poor? or your head be well fed while your body starves? Again, think of its bearing on prayer. Could a bank clerk say to a customer, "It was only your hand wrote that check, not you," or, "I cannot pay this sum to your hand, but only to yourself"? No more can your prayers, or mine, be discredited if offered in the Name of Jesus (i.e. not in our own name, or for the sake of Jesus merely, but on the ground that we are His, His members) so long as we keep within the extent of Christ's credit—a tolerably wide limit! If we ask anything unscriptural or not in accordance with the will of God, Christ Himself could not do that; but, "If we ask anything according to His will, He hears us, and we know that we have the petitions that we desire of Him."

The sweetest part, if one may speak of one part being sweeter than another, is the rest which full identification with Christ brings. I am no longer anxious about anything, as I realize this; for He, I know, is able to carry out His will, and His will is mine. It makes no matter where He places me, or how. That is rather for Him to consider than for me; for in the easiest positions He must give me His grace, and in the most difficult His grace is sufficient. It little matters to my servant whether I send him to buy a few cash worth of things, or the most expensive articles. In either case he looks to me for the money and brings me his purchases. So, if God place me in great perplexity, must He not give me much guidance; in positions of great difficulty, much grace; in circumstances of great pressure and trial, much strength? No fear that His resources will be unequal to the emergency! And His resources are mine, for He is mine, and is with me and dwells in me. All this springs from the believer's oneness with Christ. And since Christ has thus dwelt in my heart by faith, how happy I have been!

I wish I could tell you, instead of writing about it. I am no better than before (may I not say, in a sense, I do not wish to be, nor am I striving to be); but I am dead and buried with Christ—aye, and risen too and ascended; and now Christ lives in me, and "the life that I now live in the flesh, I live by the faith of the Son of God, Who loved me, and gave Himself for me." I now believe I am dead to sin. God reckons me so and tells me to reckon myself so. He knows best. All my past experience may have shown that it was not so; but I dare not say it is not now, when He says it is. I feel and know that old things have passed away.

I am as capable of sinning as ever, but Christ is realized as present as never before. He cannot sin; and He can keep me from sinning. I cannot say (I am sorry to have to confess it) that since I have seen this light I have not sinned; but I do feel there was no need to have done so. And further—walking more in the light, my conscience has been more tender; sin has been instantly seen, confessed, pardoned; and peace and joy (with humility) instantly restored: with one exception, when for several hours peace and joy did not return—from want, as I had to learn, of full confession, and from some attempt to justify self.

Faith, I now see, is " the substance of things hoped for," and not mere shadow. It is not less than sight, but more. Sight only shows the outward forms of things; faith gives the substance. You can rest on substance, feed on substance. Christ dwelling in the heart by faith (i.e. His Word of Promise credited) is power indeed, is life indeed. And Christ and sin will not dwell together; nor can we have His presence with love of the world, or carefulness about many things."

And now I must close. I have not said half I would, nor as I would have I more time. May God give you to lay hold on these blessed truths. Do not let us continue to say, in effect, "Who shall ascend into heaven, that is to bring Christ down from above." In other words, do not let us consider Him as afar off, when God has made us one with Him, members of His very body. Nor should we look upon this experience, these truths, as for the few. They are the birthright of every child of God, and no one can dispense with them without dishonor to our Lord. The only power for deliverance from sin or for true service is - **CHRIST.**

Your own affectionate brother,

J. Hudson Taylor

Now you might be thinking, *what does this letter have to do with anything concerning where I live and move in my Christian walk?*

Check this out. I want you to notice these all-consuming words of Taylor:

"They are the birthright of every child of God, and no one can dispense with them without dishonor to our Lord."

What is he talking about? *"They"* is referring to what exactly? Is it referring to our new life in Christ and all that it includes? What does it mean to have a changed life? And what does it mean to enjoy an – *exchanged life?*

I want you to hear from another choice servant of the Lord's who also served in China almost a century ago - *Watchman Nee.* Nee does a masterful job distinguishing between the two. Listen to what he says. It will bring noticeable eagle eye vision to your spiritual eyes so that you can begin to see and understand this monumental spiritual truth maybe for the first time in your life. Your Christian life and walk can never be the same.

Nee says: *"A sister once asked me about the difference between a change and an exchange.* I illustrated it with an old Bible. If we want the Bible to change, we have to give it another cover and add glue to the spine. Perhaps we can put new gold foil on the cover. If letters are missing from the pages, we have to make them up. If places have become blurred, we have to trace in the original words. After so much work and so many days, we still cannot be sure whether we have changed it the right way. But if we exchange it for a new one, we can do it within a second. All you have to do is give the bad one to me, and I will give a good one to you. Then everything is done. God has given us His Son. There is no need for us to strive for anything. Once we make the exchange, everything is done!

Nee continues: A few years ago, I bought a watch. The company that sold the watch put a two-year warranty on the watch. But the days that the watch was in the shop were more than the days it was in my home. Every few days the watch would break down, and I had to send it back to the shop for repair. This happened repeatedly. I went to the shop once, twice, even ten or more times. Eventually, I was exhausted. The watch was repaired over and over again, but it was never quite fixed. I asked the company if I could exchange it for another watch. The company said that it could not offer an exchange; it could only repair the watch, but it was never fixed. I became so exhausted that eventually I said, "You can have the watch. I do not want it anymore." The human way is the way of constant repair. During the two years that I owned the watch, it was constantly under repair. With the human way, there is no exchange; there is only the way of repair.

Even in the Old Testament, we see that God's way was not to repair or to change, but to replace. Isaiah 61:3 says, *"To appoint unto them that mourn in Zion, to give unto them beauty for ashes, the oil of joy for mourning, the garment of praise for the spirit of heaviness; that they might be called trees of righteousness, the planting of the LORD, that he might be glorified."* God's way is the way of replacement. God does not change the ashes. Rather, He replaces the ashes with a headdress. He does not change the mourning. Rather, He replaces the mourning with gladness. ***God's way is never to change, but to exchange.***" (End Quote)

How's that for seeing the Christian life as it really is? My guess is - *This landmark biblical truth is undoubtedly a lot different than what you have been taught or even walked in.* Jesus reminds us all that it is the truth that sets us or make us – free. Free to be what God had planned at first. The devil and his minions have for too long kept the body of Christ in bondage on a daily basis. When the best day we have during the week is Sunday, something is wrong. The Head of the Church means for us to be delivered from sin and temptation on a daily basis not just on the Lord's day. And Christ wants us to be free indeed longer than it takes for us to leave our seats in church and place our bottoms down for lunch at the local restaurant.

The Exchanged Life Discussed

"Not I, but Christ" seems to sum up perfectly the exchanged life in Christ. Enough of us have heard many times 2 Corinthians 5 and verse 17 quoted.

"If any man [woman] be in Christ, he [she] is a new creature [creation], old things have passed away and behold, all things have become new."

This verse was taught to me as it was undoubtedly taught to you as the key verse is the essence of a **changed** life in Christ. It is not. And why not? Simply because it is more accurately describes the reality of an **exchanged** life in Christ and both cannot be in play here. Follow the Holy Spirit's logic with me for a moment.

If we are in fact *"in Christ"* and we become a *"new creation",* then this must mean that we are not the same as we once were. But not only that but it also communicates to us that we have left one life behind for the adoption of a new life, which is biblically understood to be infused and in the realm of Jesus Christ. That is why it says, *"old things have passed away"*. Notice "the old" hasn't been changed or reformed or even transformed but they are gone and have become ancient history. We learn from history, but we cannot successfully - *live by it.* So, it is with the new life that we enjoy in Christ. Jesus thought we were [*in Adam and in ourselves in our sinful condition*] so bad and unredeemable that he not only crucified the old us but more importantly – *He replaced the old us - with Himself.* This is the linchpin and the essence of the Christian life. *"Not I, but Christ"* as Paul puts it.

When you became a believing sinner, a great exchange took place. Jesus Christ took your place and died for you on the cross. All of your sins were placed upon Jesus Christ, and He died in your stead. In that great transaction, Christ willingly took all your sins and guilt, and in "exchange" you received His righteousness as your eternal position in Christ.

The Apostle Paul expressed this great spiritual principle in the following words. "He (God) made Him (Christ) who knew no sin to be sin on our behalf, that we might become the righteousness of God in Him" (**II Corinthians 5:21**).

The core of the **Exchanged Life** is, *"His life for mine and now my life for his."* Many Christians get the first part of that statement but stop short of the second half to their own peril and loss.

This is what the apostle Paul was saying in 2 Corinthians 5:15 when he wrote, *"And he died for all, that those who live should no longer live for themselves but for him who died for them and was raised again."*

Christ died yes, but now lives. Not only is he seated at the right hand of the Father but, because of the nature of the gift of Holy Spirit he has given us, he can now live on earth through us. *(www.truthortradition.com/articles/the-exchanged-life)*

An *illustration* that I once heard would be helpful at this point.

If I take a 3x5 card and place it between the pages in my Bible that card becomes a part of my Bible. Regardless of where I take my Bible it goes with it. If I lay my Bible down somewhere that 3x5 card goes with it. If I lose my Bible, I lose the 3x5 card. The card is now a part of my Bible. In the same way, I am now so identified with Jesus Christ through His death and resurrection, and the new life the Holy Spirit has imparted to me that I am in Christ. I go with Him wherever He goes.

CONCLUDING THOUGHT

The fact is, if you are saved by the grace of God, your old life - what you were in Adam, has been replaced or exchanged for a new life – that which you are in Christ Jesus. Keep in mind that this cardinal truth of scripture has nothing to do with how you feel, what you believe or have believed to this point or what others tell you along the way. It is true because it is God's specific word to you that not only works but must be accepted and applied so that your Christian life may be one of thriving and not just hanging on by a thread until Jesus rescues you. That is not why Jesus died and that is not why you live.

4

Sin Conscious or Saint Conscious?

SATAN SAYS: LOOK AT YOUR SIN

GOD SAYS: LOOK AT MY SON

"Therefore, do not let sin reign in your mortal body, that you should obey it in its desires. And do not present your members as instruments of unrighteousness to sin but present yourselves to God as being alive from the dead, and your members as instruments of righteousness to God. For sin shall not have dominion over you, for you are not under law but under grace." -Romans 6:12-14

"I'd rather laugh with the sinners than cry with the saints." -Billy Joel

When I was new to the Christian faith, I was sorely enamored with my own sin and the great cloud of temptation(s) that seem to hang over my heart daily. It seemed that I could hardly go an hour without being assaulted and worked over by the author of sin and it proved to be rather exhausting in every way. I hate to admit that I continued for a few years in that pitiful state and no matter what I did on the religious front, nothing helped in any significant way. When I would talk to well meaning spiritual leaders they would tell me the same old advice: *Read the Bible more earnestly, pray more regularly, attend church and Bible studies more faithfully* and a host of other *"schemes"* that would certainly help me stem the tide of the fiery darts of the wicked one and give my mortal flesh a fighting chance. Hum?

I have some interesting and definitive news. ***This kind of shotgun strategy did not work and how could it really?***

You read that last statement correctly. Not that reading the Bible more or praying more or being in the company of other Christians wasn't good and even desirable because it was and always is. It just wasn't the way I (or you) receive spiritual relief at the core level of our being. You might say, ***why not, Chris***? Well, it simply does not jive with the way Christ has provided for each of His children. In this chapter and in the chapters to come, I will share with you how I got real victory, deliverance and freedom from sin's power in my life for the foreseeable future. Stay tuned. You don't want to miss this.

It can be said that - *The Christian life* and the work of Christ on our behalf can be reduced to this simple summary:

*God has **[past tense]** saved us from the **penalty** of sin – the biblical term for that is being **justified**; being declared perfectly righteous before God in Christ.*

*God is saving **[present tense]** us from the **power** of sin –the biblical term for that is sanctification; being increasingly set apart for God's use.*

*God will **[future tense]** save us from the **presence** of sin – the Bible describes as the process of glorification; being seated in the heavenlies with Christ in actuality forever.*

Pretty helpful ha? Now, it is important to note that - *Sin itself is not dead in this world or in our Christian life as we sadly know all too well.* So, it seems likely that we are saddled with its power and bite until we are finally translated out of this sinful world. But that certainly is not the end of the story as we will see. You will be surprised and encouraged at our findings.

When we talk about sin, the question is, ***do we in this world (and even in the church) even know what "sin" is anymore?***

In an age where sin has been replaced with buzz words like, *'disease, weakness and shortcoming'*, we are at a great disadvantage to measure sin for what it is. We need to still remind ourselves that God still calls sin – ***sin!*** He has not changed in His person and neither has his standard of righteousness changed, even if we often act as if it has and live accordingly.

So, what is sin exactly? I love what Pastor John Piper says sin is in by its very essence: It is...

- *The glory of God not honored.*
- *The holiness of God not reverenced.*
- *The greatness of God not admired.*
- *The power of God not praised.*
- *The truth of God not sought.*
- *The wisdom of God not esteemed.*
- *The beauty of God not treasured.*
- *The goodness of God not savored.*
- *The faithfulness of God not trusted.*
- *The promises of God not believed.*
- *The commandments of God not obeyed.*
- *The justice of God not respected.*
- *The wrath of God not feared.*
- *The grace of God not cherished.*
- *The presence of God not prized.*
- *The person of God not loved."*

Well done. That pretty much sums it up, doesn't it? Put another way, someone described sin this way:

Sin is ...the willful transgression or neglect of God's holy law...His Word.
Sin is ...selfishness in attitude and action. It is loving self-more than you love God and others.
Sin is ...saying, "My will...not Thine...be done."
Sin is ...falling short of the glory of God (Romans 3:23).
Sin is ...brought to life in greed, deceit, covetousness, lust, hatred, and idolatry.

Sin is ...your deadliest, most poisonous, most untrustworthy enemy.

Sin is ...waiting like a hidden sniper looking to ambush and destroy you.

Sin is...what will wreck your life, break up your marriage, and tear your home apart.

Sin is why God in Christ came to a cross and rose again the third day.

I think you get the picture. Sin is ugly and evil to the perfect holiness of the Lord Jesus Christ and it must be to us. But what does sin have to do with us now that we are children of God? Good question.

The trillion-dollar question is this*, how do you presently defeat sin and temptation in your life? How does it really happen so you and I can see spiritual victory in our lives and not just talk about it?*

I want to discuss this important distinction for the rest of the chapter. Buckle up. Your in for a real treat.

Sin Consciousness or Saint Consciousness?

So, what is being sin conscious exactly?

Jim Reish explains it like this, *"It is when you are always conscious of sin and feel you need to be forgiven. When we ask for forgiveness and we do not accept the forgiveness offered by God, that is when sin consciousness becomes a problem. When God forgives you, you must receive that forgiveness and then forgive yourself. If you don't, then you will not forget the sin you committed, and your mind will be on it. As a result, you will feel wrong and you won't have confidence with God. And when we don't feel right with God, our prayers are ineffective because we feel like we don't have a right to have our prayers answered. Sin consciousness robs us of our righteousness. Although God made us righteous, if we do not accept it then we still feel wrong."*
(Source:https://www.jimandjanean.com/home/2020/5/31/freedom-from-sin-consciousness

I have, more than a few times, been called *an **Antinomian or a purveyor of Antinomian teaching*** partly because of what we are going to talk about for the rest of this chapter.

For those of you who have no earthly idea (which I am quite sure is most of you) what that charge being leveled means, let me spell it out to you.

The word *antinomianism* comes from two Greek words, *anti*, meaning "against"; and *nomos*, meaning "law." *Antinomianism* means "against the law." Theologically speaking**, *antinomianism*** is the belief that ***there are no moral laws God expects Christians to obey***. Since Christ has fulfilled the law, the Antinominalist says that grace rules the Christian and he no longer must be pressured to obey God's commands.

Ryan Reeves, in an article for Gospel Coalition, quotes Martin Lloyd Jones in his work on the Book of Romans when he says, *"If you preach grace well, you will at times sound Antinomian."* I will be the last to admit my expertise on understanding the grace of God, but I hope that you see by the chapter's end, the profound teaching of God's grace as it relates to the Christian life more than ever. If that means, I am an Antinominalist, sign me up. Having said that, let me go on record as seriously saying that in the truest sense, I do not believe I am, nor do I wish to be at any point in my walk of faith.

With that in mind, I certainly understand we are all (*none spared*) riddled with this body of flesh that centers around me, myself and I. I also am aware of what the apostle John said in I John 1 - *If we say we have no sin, we call him a liar.* I am not at all saying we do not sin. I am not saying that we do not even have a propensity to sin and choose its path rather passionately on a regular basis. What I am saying is there has been a change when it comes to dealing with sin as a child of God that has been not so easily portrayed or proclaimed from our churches and the result has been defeat, shame and a major hit on the veracity of Christianity all around the world. That's a mouthful but it is nevertheless the real deal.

The question at the end of the day is, ***does it help us as believers in Christ to constantly be enamored by temptation and sin and to live with a defeatist attitude before we get out of the church parking lot?*** Sin conscious or saint conscious? We can't be both and at the same time, glorify the Lord who bought us with His own precious blood. Something has got to give.

I want to discuss what the Newer Testament says about sin and sainthood. I wrote about this in my first book, ***The Identity Driven Life*** and I do not believe in re-inventing the wheel so forgive me for sharing this section with you from the book. It will bring to focus what and where we need to travel in our relation to spiritual freedom.

Since believers in Christ are called "sinners" *once* in the New Testament, does that mean *that God minimizes sin in the life of the believer?* I love what Paul says in response to this question, *"Shall we continue in sin so that [God's] grace will increase. May it never be. (In another words, kill the thought) How shall we who died to sin live any longer ruled by it."* (Rom. 6:1-2 – Gregas paraphrase) Yet isn't it interesting that the Holy Spirit (the Divine Author of the scriptures according to 2 Tim. 3:16-17) does not label us as active, positional "sinners" more than once. I bet (like me) you thought it was a lot more. It is true that many preachers (of which I was formerly one) seem to be fixated on the potential and power of "sin" when they speak to the peeps and I am not fully sure why? I mean I have some good theories of why I think we love to make the sheep squirm, but I would only be inciting a riot in our churches if I shared them. That's never good! (Lol)

Again, I don't want you to miss the big picture here. *Do I believe that Christian's sin?* Of course, I do. 1 John 1:8-10 clears that up for us without argument. *Do I believe that Christians can live "ugly" lives at different times in their life as they make their way to Heaven?* I have unfortunately seen this far too often and besides its reality is clearly supported by the scriptures. *Do I believe that the scriptures teach true and real "repentance" is needed for Christians as well as unbelievers?* Yes, I do, and I am willing to bet that most of us reading this book have very little understanding and exposure with the term "repentance" let alone its powerful implications in our walk with Christ. It is a sign of the times in our churches to be ignorant of its need and power.

I go back to the question I asked earlier. *How many times does God call us, we who are His children, "sinners" in the New Testament? How many times does the New Testament call believers in Christ "saints" or those who are "sanctified"?*

Take a guess and don't look below. Not once, not twice, not even ten times, though would you not admit, *that ten times would be too many.*

Ready for the answer? It may floor you. It floored me the first time I heard it and then discovered it for myself. *Over 60x's in the King James Version of the New Testament.*

Say what, say what? Can you believe that? It is hard to swallow but it is the complete truth. You may be say, *"I can't believe it."* Well, I hate to break it to you but just because you can't or won't believe it, doesn't negate its truth one centimeter. You see, our feelings, our doubts or even our inability to receive this awesome truth does not weaken its divine reality in the least. Don't ever forget that God's word (His final account) is settled (fixed, completed) in heaven. (Psalm 119:89) And that is good for everyone.

What Does A Saint Look Like in The Newer Testament?

No doubt some or even many of you grew up with a religious bent towards religious "saints." You probably grew up believing that saints are *made* not *born*. I mean how many saints do you think you saw growing up? The true answer is -*a lot more than you think*. A saint too many is a person who has lived an extra ideal religious life, was a worker of miracles on some level and went straight to heaven when they passed – no questions asked. Does that sound about right? Well, you'll be happy to know that the Bible does not even remotely paint that familiar portrait. In fact, the Bible flatly rejects the idea that real saints are made by the way they live or die.

In fact, the Bible says that saints are actually "born" or reborn and not made at all. The Bible says it this way: *Saints by calling and grace, not by working or performing.* I'm going to give some of you a chance to catch your breath at this point. Ok, got it? Let's continue.

If you are still fixated on the point – **Saints are not made but born,** let me challenge your mind further for a minute so I can prove it to you and so we can wrap this chapter up on the same page.

Question: **Who were the fleshliest, misguided, childish and immature believers in the New Testament?**

And the answer. **The Corinthians believers**. They had more problems to deal with than a mathematician. In fact, Paul lays them out spiritually in both of his letters and on the surface, they have little to show for a strong Christian faith.

Yet, notice what he says to them in his first letter and chapter 1 and verses 1-3: *"Paul summoned by the will and purpose of God to be an apostle (special messenger) of Christ Jesus, and our brother Sosthenes, To the church (assembly) of God which is in Corinth, to those consecrated and purified and made holy in Christ Jesus, [who are] selected and **called to be saints** (God's people), together with all those who in any place call upon and give honor to* *the name of our Lord Jesus Christ, both their Lord and ours: Grace (favor and spiritual blessing) be to you and [heart] peace from God our Father and the Lord Jesus Christ.* **(Amplified Version)**

"Called to be saints" is what Paul says. That is who they were and that is **who we are** if Jesus knows us. That is in fact our truest spiritual identity. Sinners yes but that is not what we are by position or standing **now** that we have come out of spiritual darkness into the light of Christ! (Col. 1:13) We are saints of the living God and because we are, we can be "set apart" to do the good things that God has for us. Don't miss the order!

During a sermon, a pastor asked a reflective question to the congregation, *"And what is a saint?"* A little boy looked up at the stained-glass windows of the apostles and blurted out, *"People who let the light shine through!"* **(Source:Kent Crockett's SermonIllustrations, www.kentcrockett.com)**

Why not? That is who we really are!

History tells the story of Abraham Lincoln, who one day went to a slave auction and noticed a rather attractive black woman who was about to be auctioned off. So he began to personally get into the bidding. The bidding went back and forth until finally he had purchased her. They brought her over to him, and he instructed them to take the shackles off her wrists and ankles. Then he said to her, "You are free to go."

She looked at him and said, "You mean that I don't have to go home with you?" He said, "No, you don't." She said, "You mean that I don't have to do what you tell me to do, or say what you tell me to say?" "That's right." "You mean I don't have to be your slave, I don't have to put up with your whims and your fancies?" He said, "No, you don't. You are free to go."

She bowed her head, and tears started coursing down her cheeks. She looked up at Abraham Lincoln and said, *"Then I guess I'll go with you." (Message: Overcoming Sin by Robert Walker, Sermonsearch)*

As we close this chapter, this story illustrates with great force that which Christ accomplished for us when he freed us from sin's slave market. We are always quite aware of how evil we can be without walking daily in the Spirit but although we are not what we ought to be, we certainly are not what we use to be. The Christian life was meant to be lived with all the facts. The facts are you are no longer labeled a sinner but a saint. Not because you feel like it. Not because you are always living up to it but because it has been eternally declared by the God who makes the calls in these matters. Christ blesses us on the front end with the desire to see us respond in humility and gratitude on the back end.

The balls in your court. What kind of mindset are you going to have from this chapter on? I think you know the answer to that!

Closing Prayer: *"Dear Father, I thank you for sending your Son, Jesus, to die and shed His blood for the remission of my sins; I'm cleansed and purified. I walk in the finished works of Christ. Therefore, there is no condemnation for me. I am justified, free from the accusation of the evil one, in Jesus' Name. Amen."*

5

Not I, But Christ: What Does That Mean?

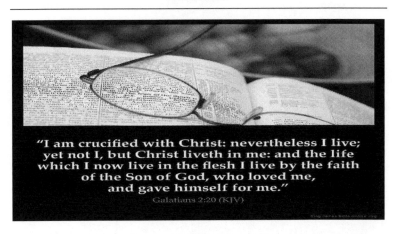

"I am crucified with Christ: nevertheless I live;
yet not I, but Christ liveth in me: and the life
which I now live in the flesh I live by the faith
of the Son of God, who loved me,
and gave himself for me."
Galatians 2:20 (KJV)

*"If Christ is in us, what will be the consequences? Why,
He will put us aside entirely. The I in us will go. We will
say, "Not I, but Christ." Christ undertakes our battles for
us. Christ becomes purity and grace and strength in us."*
-A.B. Simpson

*"The true Christian life is not so much a believer's living
for Christ as Christ's living through the believer. Because
in Christ "all the fulness of Deity dwells in bodily form",
the fulness of God also dwells in every believer, as
"partakers of the divine nature". I do not have such a
divine life and the magnanimous privilege of being
indwelt with the living, powerful Son of God because of
anything I have done or merited, but only because He
loved me, and delivered Himself up for me."*
-John MacArthur

The story is told that when the great saint of old, **Augustine,** was still without God and without hope in this world, the Holy Spirit convicted him on the basis of Paul's words in Romans 13:14, *"But put on the Lord Jesus Christ, and make not provision for the flesh, to fulfill its desires."* Augustine acknowledged his sinfulness, accepted Jesus as his Savior, and became a different person. His entire outlook on life began to change because of his new nature.

One day he had to attend to some business in his old digs in Rome. As he walked along, a former companion saw him and began calling, *"Augustine, Augustine, it is I!"* He took one look at the poor, disreputable woman whose company he had formerly enjoyed, and he shuddered. Reminding himself of his new position in Christ, he quickly turned and ran from her, shouting, "It's not I! It's not I!"

Augustine had found the secret of Paul's words: *"I live; yet not I, but Christ lives in me"* (Gal. 2:20). *(H.G Bosch, Our Daily Bread, Copyright RBC Ministries, Grand Rapids, MI.)*

The bumper sticker **"Jesus is my co-pilot"** may be a well-intentioned sentiment, but it does not have any scriptural support. Whenever I'm in the driver's seat of my life, the destination is nowhere good. Jesus is not meant to be just a spiritual "co-pilot" giving directions every now and then. He is always meant to be in the driver's seat. Period! End of story. Goodbye and Amen.

The Christian life is Christ. There has never been anyone else who successfully lived this life but Him. And He continues to do that one Christian at a time as He has full compliance to do so. Somewhere along the line, we learned that to live for Christ is up to us entirely. It is not even remotely. Yes, we must obey His commands. Yes, we might allow Him to lead. Yes, we must be renewed in the spirit of our mind by the word of God but no life that is supernatural can come from we who are natural and earthly. It is a divine life, or it is none at all and we must come to realize that we can never pull off that which is supernatural in nature.

We must come to realize that Christ saw our hopeless state in such vivid color, that He did not choose to reform us or renovate us but - replace us entirely. That is what we call the "exchanged life." It is not really a changed life as much as it is an exchanged life. We were so pitiful in our fleshly and unsaved state, God decided to get us out of the way entirely. Now our body is a host for the Son of God to work His divine magic in us first and then through us last. Jesus is not along for the ride. It is the exact opposite. We are His workmanship created in Christ Jesus for good works - His good works which become our good and eternal works. To God be the glory!

Today, ask yourself the question, *am I completely yielded to the work of Christ in me and through me? Have I given up the reigns of my life and handed over to the One who can make something out of nothing? Am I, by faith, trusting the Son of God to use me so that others might know how good He really is?*

Breathe a sigh of relief today. It is not up to us to do the work. It is God who works in us both to will and to do of His good pleasure. (Phil. 2:13) That means exactly what it says. From start to finish, it is Christ in us the hope of glory. When you and I understand this and begin to rest in its beauty, the Christian life no longer becomes a life to endure but enjoy. That is what God is after in our lives. That is what Satan fears and tries to keep us from our whole life. You must know the truth because when you do, the truth will make you free - said, Jesus."

We must realize that getting spiritually free and staying spiritually free has to be the highest desire we can have in this world where spiritual bondage and slavery is free for the asking and unfortunately - not in short supply.

An Intimate Look at Galatians 2:20

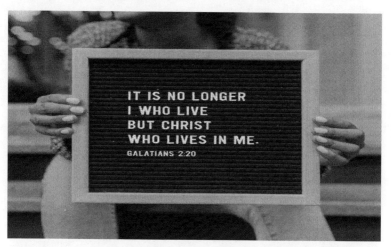

Not I, But Christ: What Does That Exactly Mean?

I am relatively sure that you have heard **Galatians 2:20** at least once or maybe not. I want to spend the remainder of the chapter breaking this verse down so that you can understand more deeply and profoundly the great goal that Christ has for our lives. In this verse, we capture the essence of the Christian life. Isn't it worth knowing this "essence"? I thought so.

I have been crucified with Christ. It is no longer I who live, but Christ who lives in me. And the life I now live in the flesh I live by faith in the Son of God, who loved me and gave himself for me. (ESV)

Let's chop this up a piece at a time. It may be the most liberating study you have ever been a part of.

"I have been crucified with Christ,"

The first thing we notice about this phrase is that it is – *past tense*. *"I have been."* In other words, it has been already accomplished with continuing results. That is how the original language (Greek) translates it. It is not something that is going to happen or even needs to happen as if we ourselves had a hand in seeing this happen. It is has happened and it was done by God – once for all, for every believing sinner. What do we do when something has already happened? We accept it and act accordingly. The fool and the ignorant try to accomplish something that has already been done and finished completely.

The second thing is we died spiritually. It says we have been *"crucified"*. Now most of us know that Jesus was crucified but what does it mean when Paul says, we have been crucified? In Romans 6, Paul tells us that the same way and at the same time Jesus was crucified, we were, spiritually speaking. In other words, when Jesus died, we died. Our old self (*in my case, the old Chris Gregas)* that who we were before we came into a new relationship with God through Christ, was, once for all, put to death so that the old us would be rendered powerless spiritually speaking.

Lastly, we have died – *"in and with Christ."* That is the most important part of this first phrase, in my humble opinion. We did not die ourselves. We died in and with Christ. Which means that all that He did to die and be buried only to rise to newness of life is our inheritance as well. **(Romans 6:3-13)** Paul says that we died to sin once and now we live to God. The apostle John reminds us that, *"As Jesus was in this world, so are we."* **(I John 2:6)**

Unless our spiritual death to sin is tied to the work of Christ on the cross, our death can never yield the fruit of a new life, one which can say no to sin based on the freedom every believing sinner has been afforded.

"It is no longer I who live,"

Say what Paul? I must admit that when I first read this, I thought, does this guy have a clue? It seems a very strange to say, "It is no longer I who live." When it obvious that he is alive because he is writing this. But let's unpack what the Holy Spirit would have us understand with this statement. It is groundbreaking.

First, **we as Christian's no longer live as it relates to our old self.** Paul is not saying we do not live anymore but the radius and scope of our living is no longer the way it used to be in our unsaved state. *Why?* Because our old self has been once and for all – crucified and put to death by the cross work of Jesus Christ. What does that mean? That the old Chris Gregas, B.C. (before Christ) is dead and gone. There is nothing I can do to bring him back. When I truly realize what I was before I knew Christ, why would I ever want to bring him back? That life is no life at all and there is nothing we can do to change that. That is why Christ gave it the deep six. We may not practically live this truth out on a daily basis, but it does not change the reality of it and its secure transaction.

Second, **our Christian life is not to be lived by our own strength or in the power of our old self or life.** In other words, the way we lived life before Christ can never work or be acted on after we come to know Christ. It doesn't work simply because what was the standard before is not the standard now. In fact, that is what Paul says in Romans 6:14 when he writes, *"You are no longer under the [rule] law but under [the rule] of grace."* Grace is always a higher standard than the law which means there is more responsibility on us because we have **Someone** else who is able and willing to live this life, we call Christian. That Someone is of course, Jesus Christ. That is what is meant by the next phrase of the verse.

The figure of the Crucified invalidates all thought which takes success for its standard. –Dietrich Bonhoeffer

"but Christ who lives in me,"

Not I, but Christ - beautifully sums up the Christian life. There can be no easier way to understand the Christian walk and experience than in those four simple words. Look at the following verses about Christ taking residence in our hearts.

"When Christ, who is your life appears, you will appear with Him in glory."
"Or do you not realize about yourselves that Jesus Christ is in you?"
"For it pleased God...to reveal His Son in me."
"Christ in me, the hope of glory."
"My children, with whom I travail again in birth until Christ is formed in you."
"That Christ may make His home in your hearts through faith."

Reflecting on Galatians 2:20, Donald Guthrie says, *"Paul thinks of himself as having become so closely identified*

with Christ that Christ dominates his whole experience."
...he thinks no longer of carnal living pursuing the desires
and impulses of the self, but a new kind of living, a faith
life."

Toby Sumpter writes, *"There is no halfway life in Christ*
because there is no Christ who is halfway alive. There is
only life in Christ and death apart from Him. There is only
shame and guilt and sorrow and fear, or else all of that is
crucified with Christ and we live because He, being fully
alive, lives in us." (tobysumpter.com)

What is the significance of Christ living in us? What does
it mean for our Christian walk?

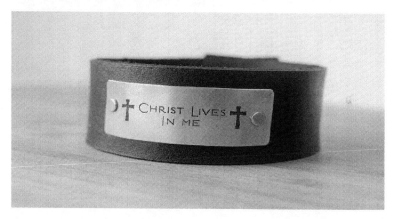

Think and meditate on the phrase again, **"Christ who lives**
in me." It does not *just* mean that Christ lives in us and His
presence comforts us. It does not *just* mean He lives within
us so that He can influence our decisions.

So, what does it mean? It means what we often don't
consider or maybe even understand. We have the
opportunity to drink deeply as this biblical treasure of a
phrase is unfolded for us. It is arguably the greatest comfort

and hope for the Christian as they make their way toward their real Home.

The great prince of preachers, Charles Haddon Spurgeon reminds us that, *"If you leave out Christ, you have left the sun out of the day, and the moon out of the night, you have left the waters out of the sea, and the floods out of the river, you have left the harvest out of the year, the soul out of the body, you have left joy out of heaven, you robbed all of it's all. There is no gospel worth thinking of, much less worth proclaiming, if Jesus be forgotten. We must have Jesus as Alpha and Omega in all our ministries."*

"And the life I now live in the flesh I live by faith in the Son of God,"

What we have here is a remarkably interesting phrase. It is translated "live by faith in the Son of God" but that is a poor translation indeed. Other translations say (which seem to sum up with the original language conveys) ***The faith OF the Son of God.*** We might say we understand what it means to live **BY** our faith **IN** the Son of God. But this verse suggests something else: We are to live **IN** the faith **OF** the Son of God. *What is this faith **OF** the Son of God, and how does one live **IN** it?*

Andrew Wommack points out, *"Paul did not say that he lived by faith **IN** the Son of God but by the faith **OF** the Son of God. The measure of faith that Paul had was the same measure that Jesus had.*

So, what is the Holy Spirit saying and how does it drive home the message of Galatians 2:20?

David A. DePra writes, *"Paul never teaches that you are I are being made to - **look like Jesus**. He never says we are to somehow acquire the character traits **of** Jesus. He never says that God or the Holy Spirit will do stuff **to us** and change us into a little version of Jesus. No. Rather, we are to manifest the Christ who is within. In other words, Christianity is NOT us acting or looking like Christ – it is Christ living **in** and **through** us. It was necessary to establish that a Christian is one in whom Christ dwells – Christianity is Christ in you, i.e., you in Christ. It was also necessary to establish that God wants to FORM Christ in us – and that in doing so, Christ will eventually be seen through us. This is all about CHRIST.*

It is not about us improving ourselves with Christian religion. The faith OF the Son of God is the result of the Son of God being formed in us, and consequently, the result of us knowing Him. God is speaking His Son to us. But if we hear Him, the end result of this is not merely a greater theological knowledge. No. Rather, it is the forming of Christ in us – a growing of Him in our hearts and consciousness.

This will result in FAITH. Faith comes to be by knowing Christ. But this faith is not out of ourselves as the source. It emerges through Christ. He is the author of faith. The faith OF Jesus Christ is not a matter of Christ taking us *over and believing FOR us. No. The faith OF Jesus Christ is the faith that is from out of Christ – it is based in our knowing Him. This is why Paul said, "The life that I now live is Christ living in me. **And that life is a life that I live IN the faith OF the Son of God.**"*

"who loved me and gave himself for me"

This phrase wraps it all up, doesn't it? Jesus grants us such a high and lofty life and position in Him, and it simply is because He loves us with a love that is indescribable. Do not miss that! What love is the Father's that He should place in Christ all the fulness of Himself and the ability to share this fulness with us. How do we know He loves us and is willing to live His beautiful life *IN* us and *THROUGH* us? Paul says, "and gave Himself for me [for us]". Wow! What is the proof of the love that God has for us? He laid down His life so that we might be raised up with Christ.

As we close this chapter, let me ask you an important question. Are you beginning to put the puzzle pieces together on HOW to live this Christian life in this world? Are you understanding more and more that it is, *NOT I, BUT CHRIST?*

The story is told that when the great missionary of the nineteenth century, Hudson Taylor, decided to go on mission to inland China, someone said to him that if he did so, he would surely die. Taylor replied swiftly and confidently, "I have already died." That was an appropriate answer for someone who believed that he was crucified with Christ and it was no longer him who lived. It would be many years on the mission field before Jesus would become His life in actuality and what a glad day that was.

Taylor is to have said, *"The work of God does not mean so much man's work for God, as God's own work through man."*

In 1900, there were a mere 100,000 Christians in China, and today there are estimated to be upwards of 180 million. Taylor reminds us that - This growth is God's work: one plants, another waters, but God gives the growth (1 Cor. 3:6). Nevertheless, it is the fruit of faithful labor. And Taylor labored longer and harder than most and that labor was sustained by his blessed union with Christ, rooted in Galatians 2:20. Praise His wonderful Name!

6

What The Devil Doesn't Want You To Know

"There is no neutral ground in the universe; every square inch, every split second, is claimed by God and counter-claimed by Satan." -C.S. Lewis

And though this world, with devils filled
Should threaten to undo us,
We will not fear, for God has willed
His truth to triumph through us.
The prince of darkness grim,
We tremble not for him;
His rage we can endure,
For lo! his doom is sure,
One little word shall fell him. -Martin Luther

A rookie lumberjack confidently started out determined to chop down more trees than anyone else. He made it his goal to beat his company's average tree count of fifteen trees a day. He was fixed day and night on this pursuit, and nothing would stand in his way.

On his very first day, he cut down ten trees. He said to himself, "That's pretty good for my first day." But on the second day, he chopped down ten again. No progress at all. Then on the third day, he managed only seven! Now he was puzzled, but not discouraged yet. He simply doubled his efforts the next day. Imagine how astonished he was when he finished with only five trees down!

Every day it got worse – no matter how hard or often he swung the ax, when each day ended, he had felled fewer trees than the day before. After two weeks of discouragement, the young man approached a grizzled old veteran. "I don't understand what's going on. I work hard every day, swinging my ax from dawn to dusk, but I keep getting less and less results. What can I be doing wrong?"

"Young fella," the old man replied after a long pause, "I can see them calluses on your hands and bigger muscles in your arms and that certainly proves you've been swinging your ax. But let me ask you something – *When was the last time you sharpened your ax?"*

Hello!

No one wants you to have a dull, ineffective spiritual ax more than Satan, the adversary of every believer in Christ. The devil is a deceiver and goes about attempting to discourage as many as he can work his dark magic with. He certainly does his best to keep people from following Jesus Christ and if that happens, then he and his demonic travel show are in the business of making us think that we don't need Christ as much as the scriptures says we do.

I want to discuss in this chapter – **what the devil doesn't want you to know.** Our list could be a mile long but I want to relate this to the *Christian life* since that is our aim in this book. You with me?

Dr. Adrian Rogers writes, *"It's always been the devil's tactic to pull the veil of darkness over his kingdom, so we'll not understand who he is. The devil knows—and military leaders will tell you—in any battle you must understand your enemy. He knows if we do not understand him or recognize him, we will not be prepared to fight and defeat him. My prayer is that God the Holy Spirit will so use this message and His Word that we'll pull away the mask, pull down the veil, and expose our adversary, the devil, for who he is." (Source: Message by Adrian Rogers, Know Your Enemy, October 1, 2017.)*

The apostle Paul was aware of the dangers Satan poses for Christians. We must follow Paul's example and *not be ignorant of Satan's devices* (2 Corinthians 2:11). This means we must understand the devil's tricks and traps and examine how he uses his key weapons in individually targeted ways to attack each of us. Let me remind you of a few important things as we talk about Satan and his desire to see you fail in your Christian walk.

First, **Satan is a liar and a murderer.** (John 8:44)

He has come to steal, kill and destroy. He is not happy until he is working and succeeding on all three fronts. He never has your best interest in mind so giving him ground and authority in your life is the height of spiritual foolishness and ignorance. Snap out of it. Satan is trying to destroy you and the ones you love – and love you. Do not let that happen!

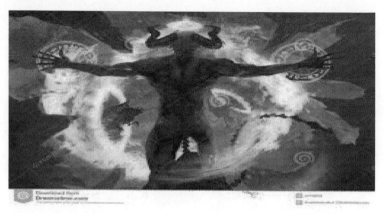

Second, *Satan wants us to be entrapped so we will do his will.*

Say what Chris? How can a Christian do the will of the devil? 2 Timothy 2:26 says, *"and they may come to their senses and escape from the snare of the devil, having been held captive by him to do his will."* The amazing thing is that even as believers in Christ, we can be captured and caged by the devil to work for him and spread his poison. That is a real bad gig to say the least. One of the chief ways we are in lock step with the enemy is to not understand or live out the Christian life in a way that pleases God. (2 Cor. 5:9) We must always remember that - *What Christ does not initiate, He does not appreciate.* Mark it down!

Then we need to understand that *the devil is always desirous to get us separated from our life, Jesus Christ.*

If the deceiver can get us out on an island by ourselves and away from our Leader, he has us, and we will be prone to looking at *ourselves* instead of the author and the completer of our faith. (Heb. 12:1-2) According to Colossians 3:4,

Christ is our life which means that He is the One who gives us what we need to live and to constantly overcome in our battle against the devil. When we are deceived in to believing that we can go it alone or feel empowered to just ask Jesus to come along for the ride, we are asking for spiritual trouble and heartache in waves. Lone Ranger Christians are always in way over their heads.

What Diablos Does Not Want You to Know...

What does the enemy of our soul want to keep us from *not knowing* about our Christian walk? What can he *accomplish* if he keeps us from understanding these simple but profound truths concerning Christian living?

Satan does not want you to know...

"Without Christ, you can do nothing."

We must always remember that - *We bear spiritual fruit; we do not produce fruit.* Yet, often we live like we are the one's producing the fruit. Jesus told his disciples literally hours before he was crucified that in order to bear fruit, real spiritual fruit that remains, we must be dependent on Him for everything because without Him, we can do nothing. In our Christian walk, we must live by this maxim: *With Jesus everything is possible and without Jesus, nothing is possible.* This is following Jesus to the max. Complete dependence and trust on Christ for everything that matters.

Our lives must be Christ-sufficient and not self-sufficient. This is the only way to bear lasting fruit that will bear dividends into eternity.

A young boy traveling by airplane to visit his grandparents sat beside a man who happened to be a seminary professor. The boy was reading a Sunday school take-home paper, and the professor thought he would have some fun with the lad. "Young man," said the professor, "if you can tell me something God can do, I will give you a big, shiny apple." The boy thought for a moment and then replied, "Mister, if you can tell me something God can't do, I'll give you a whole barrel of apples!" *(Source: https://ministry127.com/resources/illustration/god-does-the-impossible)*

If Satan can get you and I to think that we can pull it off either ourselves or with Christ's help along the way, he has defeated us before we get out of the parking lot.

Satan does not want you to know…

"Jesus is the only One that can live the Christian life successfully."

There is only one person who has ever lived the Christian life successfully or sinlessly and that is – *the One who bears the Christian name – **Christ!*** Contrary to what many of us have been taught, the Christian life is not only difficult to live – it is impossible to live. I repeat - The only person who can live the Christian life is the only one who ever lived it perfectly and that is - *Jesus Christ!* Period. End of story. And the only way you and I will experience victory as a Christian is to see His finished work on our behalf and in turn learn how to partner with Jesus by faith so that He can live His life in you, for you and through you. *This is not what Satan wants us to know or even begin to ponder.*

Satan does not want you to know...

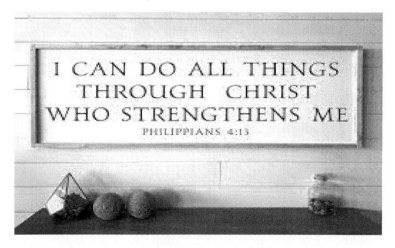

This phrase might sound familiar to you. It is the right way **(the proper Greek construction of the verse)** to quote Philippians 4:13. And in quoting it this way, it takes on a different emphasis and power. The devil would love you to read this verse in a way that most of us, in fact, actually read it and believe it. What is that? It is the emphasis on **"I"** can do all things. *"I can do all things"* becomes more about us and how God comes along side us to perform the work instead of us partnering with God as He performs His work. One says that Christ is a willing participant to what we are engaged in. The other (*which is actually the biblical teaching*) says that we, in any situation we find ourselves in, are actively involved in finding out what Christ is doing and joining Him in His work. In this model, Christ is the One who is running the show allowing us by His grace, to join Him in what He is doing as He advances His great and widening kingdom – one soul at a time.

Satan certainly does not want you to know...

"that He [Satan] was, once for all, spiritually defeated by Christ, on the cross and through His resurrection."

Satan's dirty little (really big) secret is that he still holds great power and authority over every believer in Christ. He does not and here's proof, according to the scriptures:

*And you, who were dead in your trespasses and the uncircumcision of your flesh, God made alive together with him, having forgiven us all our trespasses, by canceling the record of debt that stood against us with its legal demands. This he set aside, nailing it to the cross. **He disarmed the rulers and authorities and put them to open shame, by triumphing over them in him.** (Colossians 2:13-15 - ESV)*

*Since therefore the children share in flesh and blood, he himself likewise partook of the same things, **that through death he might destroy the one who has the power of death, that is, the devil,** and deliver all those who through fear of death were subject to lifelong slavery. (Hebrews 2:14-15 – ESV)*

*Whoever makes a practice of sinning is of the devil, for the devil has been sinning from the beginning. **The reason the Son of God appeared was to destroy the works of the devil.** No one born of God makes a practice of sinning, for*

God's seed abides in him; and he cannot keep on sinning, because he has been born of God. **(1 John 3:8-9 – ESV)**

When I saw him, I fell at his feet as though dead. But he laid his right hand on me, saying, "Fear not, I am the first and the last, and the living one. I died, and behold I am alive forevermore, and I have the keys of Death and Hades. **(Revelation 1:17-18 – ESV)**

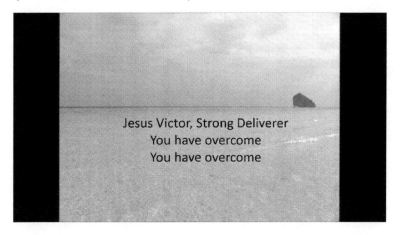

Jesus Victor, Strong Deliverer
You have overcome
You have overcome

It is clear that Jesus through His cross work and resurrection, rendered the work of Satan in the believer's life, disabled and defeated as he or she claims Christ's victory, moment by moment.

Do you think that the deceiver of the whole world – wants you to know this?

Not a chance. He wants you to think that the Christian life is *"up for grabs"* when it comes to walking in victory and Satan will do his best to keep us in the dark as to this landmark announcement by Christ and the scriptures.

7

Resting in His Beautiful Finished Work

"As long as we are seeking our worth in anything and everything but the gospel of God's grace, we will keep seeking and keep wearing ourselves out in the process. But in Christ's finished work is ultimate and eternal validation. And ultimate and eternal rest." -Tullian Tchividjian, It Is Finished: 365 Days of Good News

"We have no right to come before God at all, apart from the finished work of Christ." -R.C. Sproul

*O*nce upon a time, I, Chris Gregas, was party to a real miracle. It was a personal miracle. It is was a powerful miracle. It is was a miracle of God's own doing in a life that was terribly undone. I did not deserve this miracle. I cannot really explain adequately this divine miracle. All I can do is tell you a little bit about it and hopefully you can relate to it because it is the story of your own life. Miracles, real, amazing miracles, were made to be shared you know.

Off the coast of South China there was once built a massive cathedral. On the top of it was a huge cross that towered many feet into the air and could be seen from that South China Bay for several miles. A typhoon came and destroyed the cathedral leaving only that mighty cross towering in the air.

Sir John Bowring was once marooned in the South China Sea having been in a shipwreck. While he was being pickled in that water off the coast, he could look up and see that mighty cross as it towered in the air. The sight of the cross encouraged him because he knew he was near land. To him that cross stood for his deliverance, his safety, and his salvation. Sometime later he wrote the words to the great hymn: *"In the cross of Christ I glory, towering o'er the wrecks of time."* Towering over all the faults and the failures of mankind, above all the hurt, sin and evil things that are taking place in our world today, towering high above us all is the cross of the Lord Jesus Christ. What a privilege to preach Christ and His cross! *(Source: Dr. Tom Farrell, June 27, 2012. Ministry127.com)*

This chapter simply will explain why as Christians we *MUST* rest in the finished work of Jesus Christ. That's it but it is enough to find ourselves living in the wonder of divine blessing the rest of our days.

Defining the Finished Work of Jesus Christ

How would you define the "finished work of Jesus Christ?" Have you ever heard the term and if you have, what is your understanding of it and how does it apply to you and your Christian walk?

Here is what we know about the **PHRASE.** It is a:

Finished work and it is a work finished - by Jesus Christ.

So, let's define both – *finished and Jesus Christ* and then we will know a lot more about what our salvation entails and how important and practical it really is.

Finished

According to Merriam/Webster dictionary, the definition of *finished* are as follows:

Entirely done. Are you *finished* yet? *Brought to a completed state.* Reviewing a *finished* manuscript.

A finished job. To keep a *finished* drawing from being smeared or soiled, spray it with a fixative. *Marked by the highest quality.* CONSUMMATE. *finished* workmanship.

Synonyms: complete, completed, concluded, done, down, ended, over, over with, terminated, through, up.

When you finish doing or dealing with something, you do or deal with the last part of it, so that there is no more for you to do or deal with. That is the definition of – **FINISHED**. It is a done deal. It is completed. It is accomplished. Nothing more must be done or improved upon. It is entirely done and over.

Work of Jesus Christ

When Jesus had received the sour wine, he said, "It is finished," and he bowed his head and gave up his spirit. John 19:30 (ESV)

Before we delve into the finished work of our blessed Savior, we must ask the question, **what do the scriptures declare Jesus to be?**

What gave him the authority to say this and what was he **"finished"** with? Would you not agree that if someone is going to claim and accomplish a finished work, he or she must be willing first and able second. So, *what gives Jesus the ability and the authority to finish a work of salvation for the elect?*

First, the scriptures are wildly clear that Jesus is in fact – God, a very God. In other words, He the same as God because He is God. From the beginning, Jesus was with God, and Jesus was God. Here, the Bible establishes the inseparable nature of Jesus and the God of the Universe. They are one and the same.

"And this is eternal life, that they know you, the only true God, and Jesus Christ whom you have sent. I glorified you on earth, having accomplished the work that you gave me to do. And now, Father, glorify me in your own presence with the glory that I had with you before the world existed." **(John 17:3-5)**

Have this mind among yourselves, which is yours in Christ Jesus, who, though he was in the form of God, did not count equality with God a thing to be grasped, but emptied himself, by taking the form of a servant, being born in the likeness of men. And being found in human form, he humbled himself by becoming obedient to the point of death, even death on a cross. **(Phil. 2:5-8)**

He is the Creator, not the Creature.

There is a fair share of scholars who believe Paul's statement in Colossians 1:15 that the *"firstborn of all creation"* teaches that Jesus was a created being. But is that true? No, it is not.

Paul did not believe Jesus was created. By describing Jesus as the "firstborn over all creation," Paul is saying that he is the absolute ruler over all creation.

"For by him all things were created, in heaven and on earth, visible and invisible, whether thrones or dominions or rulers or authorities—all things were created through him and for him." **(Colossians 1:16)**

He is the God-Man. The man who was God.

C.S. Lewis eloquently defines the ***"God-man"*** this way, *"I am trying here to prevent anyone saying the really foolish thing that people often say about Him: 'I'm ready to accept Jesus as a great moral teacher, but I don't accept His claim to be God.' That is the one thing we must not say. A man who was merely a man and said the sort of things Jesus said would not be a great moral teacher. He would either be a lunatic – on the level with the man who says he is a poached egg – or else he would be the Devil of Hell. You must make your choice. Either this man was, and is, the Son of God: or else a madman or something worse. You can shut Him up for a fool, you can spit at Him and kill Him as a demon; or you can fall at His feet and call Him Lord and God. But let us not come with any patronizing nonsense about His being a great human teacher. He has not left that open to us. He did not intend to."*

The amazing parallel to the doctrine of the Trinity is the doctrine of the ***Incarnation*** — that Jesus Christ is a very God and complete man, yet one person, forever. The scriptures from Genesis to Revelation demand that we recognize Messiah and Redeemer as Creator God and Sustainer of all that is in this vast and beautiful universe.

I love what the ***Chalcedon Creed*** says about the person and nature of Christ.

1. Jesus has two natures – He is God and man.
2. Each nature is full and complete — He is fully God and fully man.

3. Each nature remains distinct.
4. Christ is only one person.
5. Things that are true of only one nature are nonetheless true of the person of Christ.

Jesus is the ***only one*** who offers and secures man's eternal salvation.

Dr. Jesus: *"I am the way, the truth and the life, no one comes to the Father, but through Me."* **(John 14:6)**

Dr. Luke: "And there is salvation in no one else; there is no other name under heaven that has been given among men, by which we must be saved." **(Acts 4:12).**

Why is Jesus, 100% God and 100% man, able to be the Savior and Rescuer of Mankind and their sin? Simply because Jesus is the – great **I AM. (John 8:58)**

In **John 10:1-18**, Jesus declared, *"I am the door of the sheep"* (John 10:7). *"I am the door. If anyone enters by Me, he will be saved"* (John 10:9). *"I have come so that they may have life and have it abundantly"* (John 10:10). *"I am the good shepherd, and I know My own and My own know Me"* (John 10:14). ***Jesus is the only Way to God – period, end of story.***

Jesus also indicated that there is one way to heaven in **Matthew 7:13-14.** Jesus warned that the gate to destruction is wide, the road broad and spacious, and that is the way most people are going (Matthew 7:13). Jesus said the path to eternal life is through a straight gate, along a narrow way that few find (Matthew 7:14).

Here is the **CONCLUSION. *Jesus is the only one that holds the power and authority to offer freely eternal salvation to the elect.***

There are ***two basic questions*** that remain.

The *first question* Jesus Himself asked His disciples. *"But what about you?" he asked. "Who do you say I am?"* (**Matthew 16:15**)

The **second question** Jesus posed to Pontius Pilate, *"What shall I do, then, with Jesus who is called Christ?"* (**Matthew 27:22**)

Resting in The Finished Work of Christ – Final Word

How do we actually **REST** in the finished work of Christ personally?

I want to share with you *three words* that are highlighted in Paul's letter to the Ephesians that characterize the finished work of Jesus Christ carried out in our own personal walk.

It is interesting to note that Paul, in the first three chapters of his letter, does not ask anything from the believers in Ephesus as it relates to their spiritual walk or deeds. He simply extols all the *manifold spiritual blessings* that we have all received in heavenly places in Christ (**Eph. 1:3-14**) and lifts and extols the standing and position of every believer before God spiritually.

The **first word** that we see the Holy Spirit highlight as it relates to the *"finished work of Christ"* is in chapter 2.

The first word is – **SIT**.

"But God, being rich in mercy, because of the great love with which he loved us, even when we were dead in our trespasses, made us alive together with Christ—by grace you have been saved — and raised us up with him and

seated us with him in the heavenly places in Christ Jesus, so that in the coming ages he might show the immeasurable riches of his grace in kindness toward us in Christ Jesus." **(Ephesians 2:4-7 - ESV)**

While the human realm encourages us to stand and to walk before, we sit, in God's economy, we are commanded to sit (spiritually speaking) in the heavenly position that God has afforded to us in Christ.

But the question is, what does it mean to be "seated in the heavenlies with Christ" and how does that prove the work of Christ has been completed? I'm glad you asked.

SIT – Seated in the Heavenlies

How can I be seated with Christ in the heavenly places if I'm still sitting upon the earth? Isn't this impossible? How can this be true? Well, simply put, the Bible says it is true, so we must believe it and rest in it because God has rested in it through the work of His Son.

I like what Jack Wellman says about this wonderful transaction: *"When a person has repented and placed their trust in Christ, they have finished all that they need to do. Any good works we do are a result of being saved not a way that we were saved for it is written, "But God, being rich in mercy, because of the great love with which he loved us, even when we were dead in our trespasses, made us alive together with Christ-by grace you have been saved- and raised us up with him and seated us with him in the heavenly places in Christ Jesus, so that in the coming ages he might show the immeasurable riches of his grace in kindness toward us in Christ Jesus" (Eph 2:4-7). When we trusted in Christ we were "made alive together with Christ." In contrast to being in Adam where we were all dead, now in Christ we have all been made alive (1*

Cor 15:22). Now we are told that we are seated "with him in the heavenly places" meaning that, like Christ, our works are done. We are not saved by works but saved for works but our works had nothing to do with our being saved. That's why we are as good as in heaven already and we are essentially already seated there with Christ because God sees things that are not yet as though they already are because in His mind, they are!"

Well said and wholly believable. Even if we cannot get our arms or brains around this beautiful work that Christ finished on the cross and through His glorious resurrection, we can revel in it and completely rest in it because it is true and it is fixed in Heaven forever. Praise His wonderful Name!

Watchman Nee in his book, **Sit, Walk, Stand**, highlights these truths more broadly. Notice some of his quotes on this idea of – **"Sitting in the heavenlies."**

"For Christianity begins not with a big DO, but with a big DONE."

"The Christian life from start to finish is based upon this principle of utter dependence upon the Lord Jesus."

"Sitting" is an attitude of rest... We only advance in the Christian life as we lean first of all – sit down."

"To sit down is simply to rest our whole weight—our load, ourselves, our future, everything—upon the Lord. We let him bear the responsibility and case to carry it ourselves."

The **second word** that we see the Holy Spirit highlight as it relates to the *"finished work of Christ"* is found in chapter 4 and verse 1.

The second word is – _**WALK.**_

**"I, therefore, a prisoner for the Lord, urge you to walk in a manner worthy of the calling to which you have been called,"** (Ephesians 4:1)

Have you ever been called to jury duty? It is a "summons," or an invitation to participate in the judicial process of your country. However, this invitation, this "calling," isn't really an invitation that leaves an option of whether or not to attend. If you know a good "calling" when you see it, you will show up for jury duty! That is the exact concept Paul used when he asked his church in Ephesus to live a life worthy of their calling. It's an invitation to participate in the Christian lifestyle, but it's not an invitation that provides an opportunity for us to decline. God expects us to walk - or live - in a Christ-honoring way the same way a judge expects you to show up when he or she "invites" you to court!

The best way to explain Ephesians 1 through 3 is _**DOCTRINE**_ or _**SPIRITUAL POSITION.**_ (**Faith**)

The best way to explain chapters 4 through 6 is _**DUTY**_ or _**SPIRITUAL CONDITION.**_ (**Works**)

Let's hitchhike on these ideas.

What does Paul mean when he says that we must **"walk in a manner worthy of our calling?"**

Now that we have learned and given the needed understanding of adopting the spiritual practice of _sitting_ in the heavenlies in Christ by faith. Now that we have been assured by God that we are already in Heaven spiritually speaking. Now that we have been given the clarion call to rest (as Christ has rested) in the finished work of Christ as it relates to our standing with God in Christ, it is now high time to – **WALK IT OUT** in our own Christian lives. Amen?

I like what Paul Tripp has to say about this Ephesian progression: *"The flow of Ephesians is not to "live up to" the Gospel, but rather "live out of" the Gospel. It's an incredibly important distinction. Instead of saying "Here's the standard...now "live **UP TO IT**" the Apostle Paul encourages the believer to "live **OUT OF**" the Gospel through the power of the indwelling Holy Spirit. A few verses prior to 4:1, Paul says "according to the riches of his glory he may grant you to be strengthened with power through his Spirit in your inner being." (Eph. 3:16). In other words, because you've been strengthened by the Spirit, you can now live in a new and different way."*

John Piper adds: *"So, think this way. **NOT**: I must have faith and love so as to be worth God's favor; **BUT RATHER**: God's favor is free, and it is infinitely worth trusting. Walking worthy of that favor means walking by faith, because faith is the one thing that agrees with our bankruptcy and God's infinite "worth." Looking to God's infinite worth for our help and satisfaction is "walking worthy of God."*

And lastly Kyle Mciver weighs in on this idea of walking out our Christian faith: *"So, we order our lives by first setting the gospel before us. By soaking our hearts and minds in our heavenly citizenship. By putting on the Lord Jesus Christ, rejoicing in Him, and dwelling on all that is true of us because we are in Him. And once we've put first things first, once we have this order right, we start walking. We walk, as Paul says in Ephesians 2, in the good works that God has prepared for us beforehand that we should walk in them. We throw ourselves into obeying all of the commands and exhortations given to us in the Bible! And when we do this, we walk in a manner that is worthy."*

Watchman Nee in his book, *Sit, Walk, Stand,* shares some quotes on this idea of – ***"Walking in a manner worthy of your calling."***

"Sitting describes our position with Christ in the heavenlies. Walking is the practical outworking of that heavenly position here on earth."

"If we only try to do the right thing, surely, we are very poor Christians. We have to do something more than what is right ... The principle is that of conformity to Christ."

"The operation of His life in us is in a true sense spontaneous... it is without effort of ours. The all-important rule is not to "try" but to "trust," not to depend upon our own strength but upon his."

"Therefore, as you received Christ Jesus the Lord, so <u>walk</u> in him, rooted and built up in him and established in the faith, just as you were taught, abounding in thanksgiving" (Col. 2:6-7).

The **third word** that we see the Holy Spirit highlight as it relates to the *"finished work of Christ"* is found in Ephesians chapter 6 and beginning in verse 10.

In understanding and applying the finished work of Christ for us, the first word is – **SIT.** The second word is – **WALK.**

The third word is – **<u>STAND.</u>**

"Finally, be strong in the Lord and in the strength of his might. Put on the whole armor of God, that you may be able to <u>stand</u> against the schemes of the devil. For we do not wrestle against flesh and blood, but against the rulers,

against the authorities, against the cosmic powers over this present darkness, against the spiritual forces of evil in the heavenly places. Therefore, take up the whole armor of God, that you may be able to <u>withstand</u> in the evil day, and having done all, to stand firm. <u>Stand</u> therefore, having fastened on the belt of truth, and having put on the breastplate of righteousness,"

As the apostle Paul begins to close his letter to the Ephesian church, he makes this appeal: *"Finally, be strong in the Lord and in his mighty power"* (**Ephesians 6:10**). The word translated *"be strong"* here actually means "be strengthened," as rendered in the New English Translation: *"Finally, be strengthened in the Lord and in the strength of his power."*

Paul has been teaching the Ephesians about their high calling of God in Christ Jesus and the life that flows from it. Sitting and resting in Christ leads to walking and trusting in Christ as we move through this life towards our real Home. Now we are to lastly **STAND** in the person and work of Jesus Christ then and now.

We might ask, *what do we stand in? What is it that we can stand and stand some more without fear of anything the devil can send our way?*

First, *we stand in the strength of Christ's might or power.* Is there anyone who is more powerful in the universe than those who crafted and sustains the universe? I think you know the answer to that.

"It's important to understand what "be strong in the Lord" does not mean. In the original Greek language, the term is a passive voice verb meaning "to be rendered (more) capable or able for some task." To be strong in the Lord does not involve building up your own strength. Believers cannot strengthen themselves in the Lord; rather, they must *be empowered* or *be strengthened*, as the Greek voice indicates. To understanding what it means to be strong in the Lord is the apostle's use of "in the Lord," rather than "by the Lord" or "of the Lord." Only when our lives are positioned in the Lord, in union with Him, do we possess the appropriate power to overcome the enemy." *(Gotquestions.org – Ephesians study)*

What do we STAND in?

Second, *we stand in the whole armor of God.* There are (7) pieces of armor in the Lord's attire mentioned in Ephesians 6:10-18. Keep in mind that the imagery of the armor is taken from the visible battle gear of a Roman soldier.
#1: Belt of Truth. A Roman soldier's belt was made of metal and thick heavy leather and was the carrying place for his sword. It also had a protective piece that hung down in the front. His belt held all other pieces of his armor together. To be fitted with his belt, meant he was ready to face action.

APPLICATION: *Truth is the belt that holds the believers' armor together as well. Ultimate Truth can be found in God's Word and in the person of Jesus Christ. (John 14:6) We must know this Truth in order to protect ourselves against our flesh, the world, and the Father of Lies. Truth grounds us and reminds us of our identity in Christ all the promises of scripture that are ours because we are children of God by the new birth.*

#2: Breastplate of Righteousness. The Roman soldier was always equipped with a breastplate. This piece of armor protected his vital organs in the heat of the battle – when he wasn't quick enough to take up his shield. The breastplate was for the quick and unexpected advances of the enemy.

APPLICATION: *As believers, we have no righteousness apart from that which has been given us by Christ. Our* *breastplate is His righteousness. His righteousness will never fail. Though we have no righteousness of our own, we must still, by His power, chose to do right. Living a life that is pleasing to Him, rooted in God's Word is powerful in protecting our heart, subduing our flesh, and defeating the enemy in his tracks in our lives.*

#3: Sandals with the Gospel of Peace. Roman soldier's feet were fitted with sandals called caligae. These sandals were made to help protect soldier's feet during their long marches into battle. They had extremely thick soles and wrapped perfectly around their ankles in a way that protected against blistering. Caligae also had spikes on the bottom to help them stand firm as they traveled. This helped them have a firm foundation.

APPLICATION: *Believers also have a firm foundation in the Gospel. As believers, we have peace in knowing we are secure in what Jesus has done for us. We have peace with God at salvation (Rom. 5:1) and we can and should experience the peace of God if we refuse to worry about nothing and pray about everything. (Phil. 4:6-7) The way you walk through life will be seen by many. When you carry yourself with the fruit of the spirt, people will stop and notice.*

#4: Shield of Faith. The Roman soldier's shield was a complex piece of armor. The shield, also called a scutum, was a soldier's primary defensive weapon. It was made of impenetrable wood, leather, canvas, and metal and could be doused in water to extinguish the fiery arrows of the enemy.

APPLICATION: *Faith is the shield of the believer. Gather with other believers in the fight of faith. The best way to band together is through the closeness of a small group. This is how the church began in the first century,*

and this is where the strongest bonds are made today.
Trusting and relying on and in God's power and protection
is imperative to remaining steadfast. When the battle rages,
we must remember that God works all things together for
our good and His glory. He is always true to His promises.
*But we must receive our daily faith to **STAND** on through*
our meditation and reading of the Bible. Only then can we
fill our tank with the truth that gets into everything that we
are as people. (Hebrews 4:12-13)

#5: *Helmet of Salvation.* The Soldier's head is one of his
most vulnerable areas. Without his helmet, one blow to the
head would prove fatal. His helmet covered his entire head,
facial area, and between the eyes. His armor would prove
useless if he wasn't equipped with his helmet.

APPLICATION: *The believer's helmet of salvation is the*
most crucial piece of armor for the Christian. Without the
indwelling Holy Spirit that enters a believer at the moment
of salvation, all other armor is useless. Salvation empowers
believers to fight. It protects us in our weaknesses. Without
salvation, there is no victory. Be intentional about feeding
your mind with spiritual food throughout the day. You are
what you eat, and the scriptures were given to digest not
just suggest.

#6: *Sword of the Spirit.* All other pieces of the soldier's
arsenal are defensive weapons, but not his sword. The
sword, a gladius, was a deadly weapon. In the hands of a
skilled warrior, he could pierce through even the strongest
armor. The sword was a key part of the battle of the
warrior. It is for us as well.

APPLICATION: *Our sword as believers - is the Word of*
God, both the written and the incarnate Word. Every other
piece of armor protects us against attacks. With God's
Word, we are truly able to fight and defeat all enemies.

Christ used Scripture to defeat Satan when He was tempted in the desert. We must do the same. Be intentional about reading scripture. As I mentioned earlier, find a time that you can dedicate reading and studying the word of God where you are free of distractions. When attacked, fight back with the Word of God. When Satan attacked Christ in the wilderness, he told him, "No - for it is written..." Use Christ's example when Satan tries to come after you. He is a defeated foe, but He does not want you to know that or remember it. (Heb. 2:14-15)

#7: Prayer. This of course is the one weapon that the Roman soldier would not readily count on. But it must be the *"ingredient"* that ties all of the other weapons of our warfare – together. In prayer, we show our reliance upon God to act and move. Our entire armor is rooted in His strength. Without His presence, we are powerless in the fight. We must fight on our knees. The One who has won the war is with us in the battle. We will see a victory when we fight in His power. There is just something powerful about getting on your knees to honor the King of Kings.

The Creator of it all is omnipresent and available to talk to you at all times. Tell Him what you are thankful for and talk with Him about whatever is on your mind. Although the war has been won, the daily battle must be fought. Thankfully, we know with every fight we face, that we have the armor and weapons to help us defeat the enemy. Remember, we do not **FOR** victory but **FROM** victory. The first says it is still up for grabs. The second says it is finished and we can stand in it in time and for eternity.

What do we stand in? What is it that we can stand and stand some more without fear of anything the devil can send our way?

First, we stand in the strength of Christ's might or power.

Second, *we stand in the whole armor of God.*

Thirdly, *we stand against the devil's schemes by not seeing people as our enemy.*

> **"For we do not wrestle against flesh and blood, but against the rulers, against the authorities, against the cosmic powers over this present darkness, against the spiritual forces of evil in the heavenly places.**

One of the greatest lessons I learned from Ephesians is that – **PEOPLE**, no matter who they are or what they are – are not my real and threatening enemy. My wife, my kids, my neighbor my in-laws and out-laws are not my contention as it relates to my spiritual life. It is the devil, that old dragon that is my (and yours) nemesis now and till we cross over.

> *"There is no neutral ground in the universe. Every square inch, every split second is claimed by God, and counterclaimed by Satan." -C.S. Lewis*

"The final enemy we must face in our sanctification is also external. We are talking about Satan, that fallen angel who has rebelled against God and has sought to enlist others in his cause. The devil is a real enemy, although many people regard him very lightly in the West today. We do not often hear of people striving mightily against Satan today, but the annals of church history are filled with stories of the saints battling against the devil and his minions.

Martin Luther, for example, wrote frequently of his battles with the devil, even claiming to have seen him on occasion. It makes sense that Luther would have such a strong experiential knowledge of the devil, for Satan loves nothing more than to attack the gospel, and Luther was at the forefront of the greatest recovery of the gospel since Apostolic times.

Honestly, Satan is likely after bigger targets than most of us, but that does not mean we are not under assault from evil spirits or demons. We know that there is a legion of demons who follow Satan's lead (Mark 5:1–20), and we will find ourselves in great spiritual peril if we are not prepared to recognize their work. Not every enemy we face has a demon behind it. Our flesh and the world need no help in tempting us to sin. Yet, Satan roams the earth like a lion, seeking to devour his prey, and we need to be aware of how he and his forces often present themselves."
(Source: Tabletalk Magazine, an outreach of Ligonier Ministries)

If we are going to successfully stand in the person and completed work of our dear Savior, then we simply cannot be ignorant of Satan's schemes and we must not be led to believe that mere humans, whoever they might be, are the real spiritual problem in our lives. They are not. "Know thy enemy," wrote military strategist Sun Tzu in the 5th century BC. He is right on. In our spiritual wrestling with the "spiritual forces of evil" (Eph. 6:12), we would be wise to know our enemy and know him well. **Ignorance is bliss** does not work for the growing and victorious believer.

Lastly, **we are to stand in and against all the evil of the evil one – FIRMLY and CONFIDENTLY.**

> **"Therefore, take up the whole armor of God, that you may be able to <u>withstand</u> in the evil day, and having done all, to <u>stand firm</u>. <u>Stand</u> therefore, having fastened on the belt of truth, and having put on the breastplate of righteousness."**

Would you agree that when you stand you can either stand FIRMLY or FLIMSY? The two that stand may look at first glance as standing the same but as the seconds and minutes mount, you and I discover who is strong and who is weak and frail.

The apostle Paul, the Holy Spirit says, *"having done all that you are called to do –* ***STAND FIRM****."* That means exactly what it says. There is no room for standing in Christ in a weak and beggarly manner. There is no time or place for the believer, knowing all that Christ has accomplished for them, to stand as if they are fighting with one hand tied behind their back. No, in all these things, we are more than winners through Christ who loves us. (Rom. 8:37)

As a young man Philip was kidnapped and held as a hostage in Greece. There he remained for several years. During this time, he received a military education. Then he returned to his homeland, which had conceded many defeats and had lost much land. Within five years he had become king.

Philip II of Macedon desperately needed his army to stand firm. He is remembered for two major innovations. First is the sarissa, a very long spear. Second is the re-development of a rectangular military formation used by ancient armies (known as a *phalanx*). A core of highly trained infantrymen armed with Philip's longer spears stood shoulder to shoulder in files normally eight men deep.

If they ***stood firm*** and did not *break rank,* they were virtually invincible and struck fear into the hearts of their enemies. Using this tactic, Philip united the city-states of Greece and took the city of Philippi (which is named after him) in 356 BC.

Sometimes, it seems that the Christian life is like facing a powerful enemy. It feels like an intense struggle in which another team is attempting to push us back and break down our ranks. If we do not stand firm, we fall on our backs and slide in the mud in the wrong direction. And that can never be our default position as children of the living God. Amen?

Again, Watchman Nee in his book, **Sit, Walk, Stand,** shares some quotes concerning this all-important idea of – **Standing firm in Christ in the battle.**

"We must know how to sit with Christ in heavenly places and we must know how to walk worthy of Him down here, but we must also know how to stand before the foe."

"The word "stand" implies that the ground disputed by the enemy is really God's, and therefore ours.... Nearly all the weapons of our warfare described in Ephesians are purely defensive."

"He warred against Satan in order to gain the victory.... Today we war against Satan only to maintain and consolidate the victory which Christ has already gained. Today we do not fight **for** *victory; we fight* **from** *victory."*

Final Thoughts of the Chapter

Do you remember the title of this chapter? **Resting in His Beautiful Finished Work.** In the final analysis, we do not stand in our work or accomplishments - but in His and His alone. I love what the great prince of preachers, Charles Haddon Spurgeon had to say about this *"Conquering Savior"* one day in the pulpit that he mounted weekly for several years. I close with his classic imagery of Christ's victory – and ours.

"Christ was a man of war, our glorious Joshua was he; he had come to gird on the sword, to invest him with the

armor, and to go out and battle with Satan, with sin, and with hell. It was a terrible conflict, it was a fearful battle, but he girded himself for the mighty and the solemn work, and he completed it, he finished it. He met his foes on the battlefield, confronted all his enemies, and on the cross, he destroyed — he divested death of its sting, triumphed over Satan, the grave, and hell, and as he expired exclaimed, "It is finished!" Oh, what a sublime conflict was that my brethren, when the Captain of our salvation met single-handed and overcame the powers of darkness, fought the fight, won the victory, and died, saying "It is finished!"

What a spring of comfort flows from it to the true believer amid his innumerable failures, flaws, and imperfections. What service do you perform, what duty do you discharge of which you can say, "It is finished?" Alas! not one; your service is imperfect, your obedience is incomplete, your love is fluctuating, yea, upon it all are visible the marks of human defilement and defect. But here is the work which God most delights in, "finished." "Ye are complete in him." Turn you, then, your eye of faith out of yourself, and off of all your own doings, and deal more immediately, closely, and obediently with the finished work of Immanuel. Come away from your fickle love, from your weak faith, from your little fruitfulness, from your uneven walk, from all your short-comings and imperfections, and let your eye of faith repose where God's eye of complacent love reposes, on the finished work of Jesus."

This truth alone is truly enough to live for and – die for, if need be.

8

Beggar or Appropriator: Which Are You?

"Blessed be the God and Father of our Lord Jesus Christ, who hath blessed us with all spiritual blessings in the heavenly places in Christ": "If you run over in your mind and find one single blessing with which God might bless us today, with which He has not already blessed us, then what He told Paul was not true at all, because he said, 'God hash.' It is all done. 'It is finished.' God hath blessed us with every spiritual blessing in the heavenlies! The great pity of it all is that we are saying, 'O God bless us, bless us in this, bless us in that!' and it is all done. He has blessed us with every spiritual blessing in the heavenlies." -L. L. Letgers, co-founder of Wycliffe Bible Translators

A compelling story is told of a devout king who was disturbed by the ingratitude of his royal court. One day he prepared a large banquet for them. When the king and his royal guests were seated, by prearrangement, a beggar shuffled into the hall, sat down at the king's table, and gorged himself with food. Without saying a word, he then left the room. The guests were furious and asked permission to seize the tramp and tear him limb from limb for his ingratitude. The king replied, "That beggar has done only once to an earthly king what each of you does three times each day to God. You sit there at the table and eat until you are satisfied. Then you walk away without recognizing God or expressing one word of thanks to Him." *(Source: The Beggar At The Table, Contributed by Ashton Alexander on Jun 7, 2009)*

I want to talk to you for a few minutes about being a pitiful beggar or becoming a confident appropriator, spiritually speaking – *and the vast eternal difference between the two.*

A *beggar* is one who looks for favor from others, not because he has worked for such a blessing but simply because he feels entitled to receive and be blessed. The beggar is one who is unaware of his own benefits and abilities and has become dependent on everyone else for their success and happiness. I am sure you would agree that when you consider what "begging" and a welfare mentality really fosters, it is something that the average thinking human being would never aspire to with any sense of excitement.

An *appropriator* or the one who applies the benefits that are available is one who does not spend senseless hours and time trying to receive that which has and is already available to them. They simply live out what is in fact is theirs and in front of them. No begging, only enjoying what is in fact theirs by grace.

Understanding How to Appropriate and Enjoy What Is Ours in Christ

In our last chapter, when we discussed the *"finished work of Christ"*, we were and are saying that there is nothing else that we need to do, or Christ needs to do for our spiritual salvation and living.

Someone has wisely said - **God was the being to put faith in Calvary.** That is so true. We already have what is ours in Christ. The only thing that remains is for us as His children to accept, believe, receive and live out God's wonderful grace in our lives. From our lips to God's ears.

Question: *What role does FAITH have in us appropriating all that is ours in Christ?*

For us to appropriate all that is ours in Christ, we must exercise **FAITH** in what God has said. God says to us – are you going to believe and receive what I *SAID* or are you going to trust and live out what you *SEE*?

> *"Now faith is the assurance (title deed, confirmation) of things hoped for (divinely guaranteed), and the evidence of things not seen [the conviction of their reality—faith comprehends as fact what cannot be experienced by the physical senses]." (Hebrews 11:1 – Amplified Version)*

Billy Graham tells a true story told him by a pastor he met in Glasgow, Scotland. There was a woman in this pastor's parish who was in financial difficulty and behind in her rent. So, the pastor took up a collection for this poor woman at church, then went to her home to give her the money. He knocked and knocked at the door, but there was no answer. Finally, he went away. The next day he encountered the poor woman at the market. "Why, Mrs. Green," he said, "I stopped by your house yesterday, and I was disappointed that there was no answer." The woman's eyes widened as she said, "Oh, was that you? I thought it was the landlord and I was afraid to open the door!"

The riches of God have been made available to us in Christ, yet most of us shrink back from receiving all that God eagerly wishes to place in our hands. The riches of God cannot help us until we open the door of our hearts.

Appropriation — One More Thing

Before we leave this chapter, I want to consider a biblical formula for allowing us to maximize and cement our further enjoyment of the finished work of Christ and officially giving a deep six to begging and pleading. This *"tried and true"* biblical maxim is found in **James 4:8**. Notice what is says.

"Submit yourselves therefore to God. Resist the devil, and he will flee from you."

The Bible is clear when it comes to Satan's goal for the believer. It is best described in **John 10:10**:

"The thief's purpose is to steal and kill and destroy. My purpose is to give them a rich and satisfying life."

Christ is for life. Satan (or the spiritual thief) is for death. Christ is for life and abundance. Satan is passionate about stealing from us, killing us in every way allowable and destroying us and our testimony until we graduate. We must figure out in a real sense how to neutralize Satan and demonic hosts on a *"moment by moment"* basis. The good news is, we have a formula, really many to choose from.

Breaking Down – James 4:8

Step 1: *Submit to God.*

What does it really *mean* to submit to God?

In its simplest terms it means that *we believe and trust that God's ways are better and greater than our own plans.*

If we are honest, we know how difficult it can be to surrendering to God's will for our lives. Yes, we know His general will found in His word and we often are okay when it comes to attempting to do what it says. But letting the triune God have His total way and control in our daily walk, well, that is another subject.

In all the New Testament incidences where the word *submit* occurs, the word is translated from the Greek word *hupotasso*. The *hupo* means "under" and the *tasso* means "to arrange." This word and a root of it are also translated by the words *subject* and *subjection*. The word's full meaning is "to obey, put under, be subject to, submit oneself unto, put in subjection under or be under obedience or obedient to." The word was used as a military term meaning "to arrange troop divisions in a military fashion under the command of a leader." This word is a wonderful definition of what it means to "submit" to God. It means to arrange oneself under the command of divine viewpoint rather than to live according to one's old way of life based on a human viewpoint. It is a process surrendering our own will to that of our Father's. (*Source: Gotquestions.org, How are we to submit to God*)

So how does the word or the action to submit to God allow us to appropriate the finished work of Christ in our lives? First, **we must understand that this is a COMMAND to be followed and obeyed.** This is not just a suggestion or a good idea to be considered among many other options. It is command from God and as all other commands are to be obeyed, so this edict is to be accepted and obeyed as well. God does not require us to submit because He is a tyrant, but because He is a loving Father, and He knows what is best for us. The blessings and peace that we gain from humbly surrendering and submitting ourselves to Him daily are a gift of grace that nothing in this world can compare to. We are called to daily, moment by moment, put ourselves, arrange ourselves by faith under the mighty hand of God and let Him lead us to what His purpose is not only for us but for the others we touch.

Secondly, **submission to God is not a whim experience but it is a lifestyle approach.**

Jennifer Sum comments about this lifestyle submission this way: *"It seems logical to want to follow God wholeheartedly. Yet we often feel torn and conflicted, because many "lessons" from this world teach us why we should not.*

Control - *"Decide your own destiny." (Ignore God)*
Fear - *"Seize the opportunity now. It may not come around again." (Don't wait for God's perfect plan)*
Distrust - *"Don't trust anyone." (Do not trust God)*
Security - *"Take measures to protect or secure yourself." (Do not rely on God)*

It is easy to fall for deceptions that are "so clever they sound like the truth" when we don't make it a point to learn about God's loving and perfect nature and form the *habit of submitting every aspect of our lives to God on a daily basis." (teachinghumblehearts.com, **What total submission to God looks like**)*

As we consider what it means to living the abundant life that is our heritage in Christ, we must fully believe that not only is submission to God a command, but it is logical, and a lifestyle walk that is not perfect but consistent.

Charles Spurgeon sums it up this way: *"A lack of submission is no new or rare fault in mankind. Ever since the fall it has been the root of all sin…From the moment when our mother Eve stretched out her hand to pluck the forbidden fruit and her husband joined her in setting up the human will against the divine, the sons of men have universally been guilty of a lack of conformity to the will of God. They choose their own way and will not submit their wills. They think their own thoughts and will not submit their understanding. They love earthly things and will not submit their affections. Man wants to be his own law and his own master"* **(Sermon: The Reason Why Many Cannot Find Peace)**

NOTE: Before we move to Step 2, we need to honestly understand our own foolish propensity to buck at the very thought and command to completely surrender to God's will and way daily. Amen?

Step #2: *Resist the devil.*

We have looked deeply into what submitting to God means but - ***What does it mean to - resist the devil?***

To resist means to withstand, strive against, or oppose in some manner. Resistance can be a defensive maneuver on our part, such as resisting or withstanding the temptation to sin.

Be sober-minded; be watchful. Your adversary the devil prowls around like a roaring lion, seeking someone to devour. [9] <u>Resist him</u>, firm in your faith, knowing that the same kinds of suffering are being experienced by your brotherhood throughout the world. -I Peter 5:8-9 ESV

Aaron Berry reminds us of this, *"The Christian life is a battle. Spiritual warfare is real; angels are real; Satan is real. As the sworn enemy of our Savior, Satan's greatest desire is to turn people away from Christ through his lies and deceit. For a Christian to function as if this is not a reality is a recipe for spiritual disaster. Although the Devil cannot snatch believers away from Christ (**1 John 5:18**), he is still hard at work to cause division among believers, render them ineffective in their testimony, and damage their relationship with God. Because of this reality, Christians are called to "resist the Devil." We are to stand firm and oppose the adversary of God's people."*

"And give <u>no opportunity</u> to the devil." -Ephesians 4:27 ESV

In late September 1864 Confederate General Nathan Bedford Forrest was leading his troops north from Decatur, Alabama, toward Nashville. But to make it to Nashville, Forrest would have to defeat the Union army at Athens, Alabama. When the Union commander, Colonel Wallace Campbell, refused to surrender, Forrest asked for a personal meeting, and took Campbell on an inspection of his troops. But each time they left a detachment, the Confederate soldiers simply packed up and moved to another position, artillery and all. Forrest and Campbell would then arrive at the new encampment and continue to tally up the impressive number of Confederate soldiers and weaponry. By the time they returned to the fort, Campbell was convinced he could not win and surrendered unconditionally! *Satan likes to deceive the Christian into thinking he must be a slave to sin. Once he has done that the Christian surrenders unconditionally.* (*Nightlights for Students,* Jim Fletcher, Roger Howerton)

So, if we are going to go from a mere beggar as a Christian to a strong appropriator of God's truth in our Christian walk, we must:

Submit and arrange ourselves under the control and sway of God as consistently as we can.

Resist the devil and not allow him to control our minds and our flesh in any form or fashion.

1 + 1 = 2. What is the result of 1 + 1 = 2?

Result: *The devil will flee/run. [from you]*

WARNING: If we choose to *"reinvent the wheel"* with all of this, we will be ravaged by the dark spiritual world that Jesus died to deliver us from.

What does it mean that the "devil will run?"

We cannot be under the elusion that Satan is afraid of us or runs because he is afraid. What the Holy Spirit seems to be saying is that once we submit to God and resist the devil, he has no more place or time for us, and he leaves quickly to cause havoc in another place.

Of course, a student of scripture, would recognize this pattern in the confrontation that Jesus had with the devil in the wilderness recorded in Matthew 4:1-11. Notice the progression of all of this with a special eye on verse 11:

Then Jesus was led up by the Spirit into the wilderness to be tempted by the devil. ² And after fasting forty days and forty nights, he was hungry. ³ And the tempter came and said to him, "If you are the Son of God, command these stones to become loaves of bread." ⁴ But he answered, "It is written, "Man shall not live by bread alone, but by every word that comes from the mouth of God."" ⁵ Then the devil took him to the holy city and set him on the pinnacle of the temple ⁶ and said to him, "If you are the Son of God, throw yourself down, for it is written, 'He will command his angels concerning you,' and 'On their hands they will bear you up, lest you strike your foot against a stone.' ⁷ Jesus said to him, "Again it is written, 'You shall not put the Lord your God to the test.'" ⁸ Again, the devil took him to a very high mountain and showed him all the kingdoms of the world and their glory. ⁹ And he said to him, "All these I will give you, if you will fall down and worship me." ¹⁰ Then Jesus said to him, "Be gone, Satan! For it is written, "'You shall worship the Lord your God and him only shall you serve.'" ¹¹ Then the devil left him, and behold, angels came and were ministering to him.

What did the Son of God USE to submit to God and resist the enemy of His soul? ***"It is written."*** Three words that the devil and his minions cannot stand or stand under. The word of God, the Bible, is our STAND during temptation and spiritual attack. Nothing else will do.

*What was the **RESULT** of Jesus pressing into the word of God against the enemy?* Verse 11 - ***Then the devil left him, and behold, angels came and were ministering to him.*** He submitted to God; He resisted the devil and the devil left him for another opportune time.

Someone tells the following story. *"One of the happiest men I ever knew was a man in Dundee, Scotland, who had fallen and broken his back when*

~ 113 ~

he was a boy of fifteen. He had lain on his bed for about forty years, and suffered much pain, but the grace of God was so abundant upon him, that I almost imagined that when the angels passed over Dundee, they would stop at this bedside to get refreshed. When I saw him, I asked if Satan ever tempted him, thinking of God as a hard Master, and doubting His love. "Oh, yes," he said, "many times, as I see others in prosperity, Satan says, `If God is so good, you might be rich and well.'" "What do you do when Satan tempts you?" I asked. "Ah, I just take him to Calvary and show him Christ, and His wounds, and say, `Does He not love me?' And Satan got such a scare there, hundreds of years ago, that he cannot stand it; he leaves me every time."

The *formula* for spiritual victory is crystal clear. The *formula* for casting out the beggarly attitude that is so easily is adopted by the most ardent Christian is simple:

Submit to God - Resist the Devil = He will run and leave

"The sons of the King do not conduct themselves like the devil's beggars." -John MacArthur

As we close this chapter, I want to remind you that you are equipped and commanded to rest in the finished work of Jesus Christ. There is nothing more, on His part, or yours, to improve upon or polish up. Remember, we fight **FROM** victory, not **FOR** it. You are more than a winner through Christ. Now live that way and I will see you on the other side. **CJG**

<u>9</u>

The Mortal Combat Between Your Flesh and The Holy Spirit?

"I groan daily under a body of sin and corruption. Oh, for the time when I shall drop this flesh, and be free from sin!" -Charles H. Spurgeon

"The one who sows to please his flesh, from the flesh will reap destruction; but the one who sows to please the Spirit, from the Spirit will reap eternal life." -Galatians 6:8

"Above all the grace and the gifts that Christ gives to his beloved is that of overcoming self." –St. Francis of Assisi

Self is useless in the eyes of God. That is the beginning and the end of that.

"The curse of the Christian and of the world is that self is our pivot; it is because Satan made self his pivot that he became a devil. Take heaven from its center in God, and try to center it in self, and you transform heaven into hell."

That is what the great **F.B. Meyer** said in a sermon delivered at Carnegie Hall in New York. He was dead on. What say you?

It is amazing to me how *little* information there is on the ***"self- life"*** or the ***"flesh"*** in our religious bookstores! Irreligious bookstores are filled to the brim with the subject. The church has been largely silent and unaffected by its biblical teaching for what seems like forever. Yet, God has a lot to say to us about the subject and it is needful for us to heed His words. It is matter of life and death.

I came across a book title not long ago entitled, ***"365 Steps to Self-Confidence"*** by David Lawrence Preston. How wild is that title? You might say, *'that doesn't sound so bad, Chris. Doesn't everybody need "self-confidence" and a good self-esteem to go through life successfully? Especially a Christian?'*

Well, it depends. Unfortunately, in God's kingdom, that kind of thinking simply doesn't add up. God's kingdom we must remember is an *upside-down kingdom* where the philosophy of the culture is often in direct opposition to the teachings of scripture. The Christian must agree with the apostle Paul when he wrote, ***"in my flesh dwells no good thing."*** (Rom. 7:18) That is the real deal and really the place we must start when we talk about self or the flesh.

Someone once wisely said, *"What God does not initiate, He does not appreciate."* There is a load of truth in that statement. What does the scripture mean by the phrase "*self*" and how does it show itself?

Self can be best described as the absence of God in our lives while we do what we do. It is us doing the work of God either in our own strength or blindly believing that "God is my partner, and I can handle any situation." Is that true? It is using our fleshly mind to perform the work of God or even more disturbing, it is thinking that it is up to us to accomplish the work of Christ with His assistance. No doubt Christ is there but He is more of a *"helper"* rather than our *"Life"* (Col. 3:4) and the one who is the wind beneath our wings. (Gal. 2:20)

One of the most important aspects of Christian growth is the grand day when *the Holy Spirit's reveals the flesh's place in the Christian's life.* For one to get beyond just knowing Jesus Christ as Savior into a growing, lively relationship with Him, we must first come to know – *ourselves*. The struggle of the Christian life has to do with our flesh, that which we are born with and saddled with all of our lives.

When the Bible refers to the *"flesh"* it is just not talking about the wrapping that keeps our muscles from falling off our bones. It is speaking of our evil makeup: *those desires, patterns and lines of thinking, those behaviors and attitudes that are deep within in us that are bent away from God.* When the attitudes of self-satisfaction and self-service rear their ugly heads that is the "flesh" in rare form. When we are tempted to put God second and me, myself and I first, then we prove that the flesh is king, queen and ace.

When it comes right down to it, our *self-life* is terribly out of balanced. It is all one sided. It reminds me of the Universal Tea Party. Have you heard how it goes?

I had a little tea party, one afternoon at three, twas very small, three guests in all, Just I, myself & me. Myself ate up the sandwiches, while I drank up the tea, twas also I who hate the pie & passed the cake to me.

That about sums it up. It is simply amazing how much *"self"* rules our lives even down to the minute details. But remember this: *Self-revelation always comes **before** divine revelation!* We cannot tap into God's plan specifically unless we understand it generally. Mark it down.

In short, the flesh is self-centered as opposed to being God-centered. Sin birthed this reality. A life ruled by the flesh is a life dependent on finite human effort and resources and that is just not God's way for His children.

You and I as believers in Christ have two important things in common.

First, *we both have a flesh, that which the Bible calls, "this body of sin" that we are saddled with from birth to death. It is the playground of Satan and his demons and it is the very landscape that wreaks havoc in the Christian's life in great measure.*

Second, *all Christian's have in common is that we have all been gifted with the presence of God the Holy Spirit that takes residence within us the moment we are born again of the Spirit.*

More about the self-life or the flesh later.

The Old Nature, the Flesh and The Holy Spirit in the Christian Life

In this chapter, we want to take a deep dive into what makes us – us as a fallen creature and the divine change that is wrought when we are born-again of the Spirit.

So, the question is - *What is the role of the OLD NATURE, the FLESH and the HOLY SPIRIT in the life of the believer?*

Let's first look at what the Bible calls the old nature, the old man or the Adamic nature.

THE OLD NATURE

*Do you and I as believers **still have** an old nature or a sinful nature?*

*Do you and I as believers have **TWO** natures within us?*

*Do many versions of the New Testament use the term flesh and the term old nature/self - **interchangeably**?*

These are the questions (and more) that we will answer in this chapter. When we discuss the old nature or sinful nature, we must turn to a linchpin verse that gives us quite a healthy grasp on this concept. Here it is.

> ***Romans 6:6 - We know that our old self was crucified with him in order that the body of sin might be brought to nothing, so that we would no longer be enslaved to sin. (ESV)***

What does ***Romans 6:6*** say about the old nature in the life of the Christian?

Let me share (3) of the most plausible views of what the old nature can mean in our lives. I will leave it up to you to decide what you believe the teaching of scripture is in this regard.

*#1: We still have or possess a sin nature living within us.
that conflicts with the new nature. In other words, we
have two natures equally at battle within.*

*#2: We no longer have a sin nature within us, but we have
the flesh left to battle with the Spirit. The old nature is
gone, the flesh is left and that is what causes us to sin as we
as believers - surrender to it.*

*#3: We still have the sin nature in us, but it has been
rendered powerless in our lives. In other words, the "right
and authority" of the old nature has been broken and we
no longer must serve it.*

Let us look at these individually and see which one you
believe the scriptures support. Notice I said the one **YOU**
believe is supported from the Bible. I want you to grapple
with the concept **YOURSELF** so that you can be "fully
persuaded in your **OWN** mind" as the scriptures say. Deal?

**#1: We still have or possess a sin nature living within us
that is in conflict with the new nature. In other words, we
have two natures equally at battle within.**

This could easily be argued that this seems to be the
teaching of scripture. This is certainly the prevailing
"orthodox" teaching of the church. This seems to make
sense when we realize our struggle with sin daily.

It is important to note that - *Most people believe this
teaching to be true not necessarily because the Bible
teaches this as fact but because it seems to explain why we
sin and have that propensity on a consistent basis.* The
reasoning is that - it must be the *"old nature"* that produces
sin in our lives so we must still have an old nature, the
nature we have been saddled with since birth.

What do YOU believe and why? Let's go down the road a bit, shall we?

Norm Olson writes this, *"God neither reforms nor eradicates our Adamic nature. Rather He gives a new nature to those who become His children through salvation. Thus, a believer in Christ has two natures. We must not fall into two erroneous views. One is the idea of "sinless perfection," as though the old nature is no longer present (1 John 1:8–10). People who hold to this view generally excuse their sins, calling them mistakes, shortcomings, or weaknesses. The other erroneous view is sometimes called "sinful imperfection," the thinking that "even though I'm saved, I still have a sin nature. I can't help that, so I'll just sin, and God will forgive me."*

Such thinking fails to reckon with the holiness of God and also denies the freedom we can have from sin by yielding to the Holy Spirit, who indwells the believer from the moment of salvation. If two natures were not residing inside each believer, the apostle Paul would not have had to describe the continual conflict that he and every other believer experience day to day (see Romans 7:14–25). In Galatians Paul wrote, "Walk in the Spirit, and you shall not fulfill the lust of the flesh. For the flesh lusts against the Spirit, and the Spirit against the flesh; and these are contrary to one another, so that you do not do the things that you wish. But if you are led by the Spirit, you are not under the law" (5:16–18). In the life of the child of God, the flesh and the Spirit are continually in conflict. Who we yield to at any given moment is the one who wins out."

*"If Christians still commits sins after they believe in Jesus, does that mean Christians have a sinful nature? The short answer is "**no**," but the true reason is greatly misunderstood. The Bible is very clear that your old nature died once and for all on the cross with Jesus. It's no longer*

in you. You only have a new nature – your identity in Christ. Romans 6:6 says, "Our old self was crucified with Him, in order that our body of sin might be done away with, so that we would no longer be slaves to sin. Though you and I certainly act in a sinful way, you do not have a sinful nature! You have the new nature where Jesus has made His home in you! And you have the flesh which is not the old nature or the sinful nature. Galatians 2:20 says it died and no longer lives." (Source: Gracelifeinternational.com – Christians – sinful nature)

OLD NATURE BEFORE CHRIST	NEW NATURE AS A CHRISTIAN
Separated from Christ	United to Christ
Dead	Alive
Disobedient	Obedient
Ruled by spiritual evil	Sharing in Jesus' rule over spiritual evil
Objects of God's wrath	Objects of God's affection
Walking in sin	Walking in good works
Destined for hell	Seated with Christ in heaven

Source: Mars Hill Church

As you can see - There is a real, live tension between those who believe that we no longer have an *"old nature"* and those who say we still do and the proof of it – is our personal and consistent sin.

We do not lose our sin nature once we receive Christ. The Bible says that sin remains in us and that a struggle with that old nature will continue as long as we are in this world. Paul bemoaned his own personal struggle in Romans 7:15–25. But we have help in the battle—divine help. The Spirit of God takes up residence in each believer and supplies the power we need to overcome the pull of the sin nature within us. "No one born of God makes a practice of sinning, for God's seed abides in him, and he cannot keep on sinning because he has been born of God" (1 John 3:9). God's ultimate plan for us is total sanctification when we see Christ (1 Thessalonians 3:13; 1 John 3:2). (Source:https://www.gotquestions.org/sin-nature.html)

Do you believe that this is the way it is and the teaching of scripture?

#2: *We no longer have a sin nature within us, but we have the flesh left to battle with the Spirit. The old nature is gone, the flesh is left and that is what causes us to sin as we as believers - surrender to it.*

This belief has surely been around for most of church history, but it has certainly picked up steam in the last century or so.

Listen to what **Dr. Tony Evans** has to say in this regard: *"The moment you placed your faith in Christ alone for salvation, God implanted a new nature deep within your being. This new nature, also called the new birth, is the reference point for your identity. But what I also want you to understand is that when God gave you this new nature, through which you are now alive spiritually, He also put to death your old nature. This death occurred on the cross of Jesus Christ, when He died for the sins of the world. This is why your identity as a Christian begins at the cross. A false identity leads to false growth."*

Dr. Neil Anderson says this, *"Has the sinful nature been eradicated at the time of the new birth? One cannot answer yes or no without defining terms. If someone asked, "Do you believe that the old man is dead?" the answer is yes.*

We are no longer in Adam; we are spiritually alive in Christ. If someone asked, "Do you believe that Christians no longer sin and cannot walk or live according to the flesh?" The answer is no. The Christian retains the flesh, which the editors of the New International Version (NIV) of the Bible have chosen to interpret as "old nature," and even at times, "sin nature." This has created some semantic problems when discussing the nature or natures of a Christian. If someone asked, "Do we believe that we have a new nature?" I would answer yes, because God has given me a new heart and my inner man is oriented toward God. I have become a partaker of the divine nature (2 Pet. 1:4), and "I joyfully concur with the law of God in the inner man" (Rom. 7:22). If they asked, "Are we a sinner or a saint?" I would joyfully respond, "I believe we are saints by the grace of God, and we intend to live our lives as His children in the way He intended us to live by faith in the power of the Holy Spirit."

Romans 6 – Hard to Argue We Still Have a New Nature?

In **Romans 6**, we discover the strongest passage and argument for believing that we no longer have an old nature and now have a new nature. Notice the emphasis that the Holy Spirit and the apostle Paul make about sin and the nature of sin.

*"What shall we say then? Are we to continue in sin that grace may abound? By no means! How can we who **died to sin** still live in it?" **Romans 6:1-2***

*"Do you not know that all of us who have been baptized into Christ Jesus were **baptized into his death?" Romans 6:3***

*"We were **buried** therefore with him by **baptism into death**, in order that, just as Christ was raised **from the dead** by*

*the glory of the Father, **we too might walk in newness of life.** Romans 6:4*

*"We know that **our old self was crucified** with him in order that the **body of sin might be brought to nothing**, so that we would **no longer be enslaved to sin.**" **Romans 6:6***

*"For one who has **died has been set free from sin.**"* **Romans 6:7**

*"Now if we have **died with Christ**, we believe that we will also live with him."* **Romans 6:8**

*"So, you also must consider yourselves **dead to sin and alive to God** in Christ Jesus."* **Romans 6:11**

*"For **sin will have no dominion over you**, since you are not under law but under grace."* **Romans 6:14**

*"But thanks be to God, that you **who were once slaves of sin** have become obedient from the heart to the standard of teaching to which you were committed,"* **Romans 6:17**

*"and, having been **set free from sin**, have become **slaves of righteousness.**"* **Romans 6:18**

*"But now that you have been **set free from sin** and have become **slaves of God**, the fruit you get leads to sanctification and its end, eternal life."* **Romans 6:22**

Pretty strong language and meaning found here, would you not agree? What say you?

The *first view* we discussed says that we are indeed saddled with the old nature until death, but we receive a new nature (at salvation) that helps us overcome the power and authority of the old nature.

Result: Very believable and arguably the most orthodox view of the church worldwide and even through the ages.

The *second view* says that we no longer have an old nature or sin nature and that it has died and now we are left with a new nature and a sinful flesh that needs to be subdued.

Result: A very strong argument in Romans 6 and a belief that has ample support throughout the church age with a resurgence of this belief in the last century or so.

#3: We still have the sin nature in us, but it has been rendered powerless in our lives. In other words, the "right and authority" of the old nature has been broken and we no longer must serve it.

I must admit that this particular view seems to have the balance of both views and yet it gives a just and practical way of overcoming the world, the flesh and the devil in this world.

In other words, in this teaching, we *STILL* have an old or sinful nature, but it is rendered inoperative in our lives as we choose to die to its power and authority.

Dr. Robert Jeffrees writes, *"It is wrong to deny the existence of the sin nature. You still have a remnant of it left inside of you. But an equally lethal mistake is to exalt your sin nature. And frankly, that is the thing we are in more danger of doing in the evangelical church. People say, "As long as you are in this world, you are going to have the old sin nature in you, and you will never be able to have victory over sin until you see Jesus one day." No, Paul said, you do not have to wait till you get to Heaven to experience victory over your sin nature, because your sin nature has been crucified.*

He said in Romans 6:6, "Our old self was crucified with Him, in order that our body of sin might be done away with, so that we would no longer be slaves to sin." The phrase "done away with" means "rendered powerless." When you become a Christian, your sin nature is crucified; sin has no more power over your life than you allow it to have.

How was the power of our sin nature destroyed? Paul said in Romans 6:4, "We have been buried with Him through baptism into death, so that as Christ was raised from the dead through the glory of the Father, so we too might walk in newness of life." When Paul talked about Christians being buried with Christ through baptism into death, he was not talking about water baptism. Baptism is a symbol of a spiritual reality. The spiritual reality is this: Just as Christ was crucified and buried, when we trust in Christ as our Savior, our old nature is crucified and buried."
(Source: Pathway to Victory, Dr. Robert Jeffrees, April 25, 2018)

Q. Have you or are you learning to say NO to sin and YES to Christ?

Conclusion

Now whatever view you hold or seem to lean towards, the important thing is that you are *"fully persuaded in your own mind."* Someone might be thinking, *"what is your VIEW Chris? What do you believe the Bible teaches?"*

Well, I am not going to tell you because I not only want you to believe what you believe but I also want you (as God does) to grapple with what the Bible teaches in this area. Amen?

The Flesh

The old nature. Now let's look extensively at what the Bible calls the flesh or the *"sinful flesh."*
But the question is, *what and how is the "flesh" used in the Newer Testament and how does it work in our Christian lives?*

It is important to first realize that the **FLESH** (sinful) can and is used interchangeably with the word - **SELF.** Self or the sinful flesh - can be best described as the absence of God in our lives while we do what we do. It is us doing the work of God either in our own strength or blindly believing that "God is my partner, and I can handle any situation." Is that true? It is using our fleshly mind to perform the work of God or even more disturbing, it is thinking that it is up to us to accomplish the work of Christ with His assistance. No doubt Christ is there but He is more of a *"Helper"* rather than our *"Life"* (Col. 3:4) and the one who is the wind beneath our wings. (Gal. 2:20)

When the Bible refers to the *"flesh"* it is just not talking about the wrapping that keeps our muscles from falling off our bones. It is speaking of our evil makeup: *those desires, patterns and lines of thinking, those behaviors and attitudes that are deep within in us that are bent away from God.*

Reminders Concerning the Flesh

Let me share with you some reminders or principles concerning the sinful flesh that resides within us.

First, we need to know that - *our sinful flesh has nothing good to offer us.* Yes, you read that right.

Notice what **Romans 7:18** states, *"I know that nothing good lives in me, that is, in my flesh..."*

Paul is saying that our flesh (*our 5 senses*) has **no power** to live out the demands of God. It has no power to do what God expects on a consistent basis. So, if we attempt to, in our own strength, live out the Christian life, we will crash and burn regularly and that is not God's desire for our lives. That is not why He died.

Secondly, *God's purpose was and is to never **improve** the flesh but to subject it to crucifixion.*

The sinful flesh of a man or a Christian cannot be improved upon or renovated and reformed. **Why?** Because it is terribly tainted with sin and sinful patterns. God could have chosen to **reform** it, but in His great wisdom, He chose to be subject to **crucifixion** instead!

Galatians 5:24 says, *"those who belong to Christ Jesus have crucified the **FLESH** with its passions and desires."*

I want you to notice that it says that this crucifixion has already taken place. *("have crucified")* It is, it was, a once for all transaction that we must continually stand on and walk in. We do not keep crucifying our sinful flesh. It is done on a continual basis by understanding this divine fact and work by Christ and on the behalf of us who belong to Christ Jesus.

Thirdly, *the flesh is **hostile** to God and His will.*

This is what **Romans 8:5-7** reveals, *"For those who are according to the flesh set their minds on the things of the flesh, but those who are according to the Spirit, the things* *of the Spirit. ^{6} For the mind set on the flesh is death, but the mind set on the Spirit is life and peace, ^{7} because the mind set on the flesh is **hostile** toward God; for it does not subject itself to the law of God, for it is not even able to do so."*

The flesh is not merely an enemy of God and His Spirit, but it is overtly hostile and filled with hatred toward the triune God. That is why we must be resolute when we face the sinful flesh in all its demonic stink and stain.

In his commentary on Romans, John Murray says that to be hostile to God *"is nothing other than total depravity and 'cannot please God' is nothing less than total inability."* On our own, we are so hostile to God that we would have nothing to do with Him. If He were merely to knock at the doors of our hearts, it would not be enough. To save us, He must crash through the door, for we would never invite Him in otherwise.
*(Source: **https://www.ligonier.org/learn/devotionals/mind-set-flesh/**)*

Fourthly, *those who live by the flesh **cannot** please God.*

Romans 8:8 states, *"and those who are in the flesh **cannot** please God."* (NASB)

Notice it does not say that those who are driven by the

sinful flesh may not please God. Or those who are fleshly - do not please God. It says that those who are ruled by self **CANNOT** please God. In other words, it is not possible. It is impossible. It does not compute. It is not probable or doable – at all.

Now why do I make a real deal about this principle? Simply because the pleasure of God in our lives must be a main goal of our Christian experience. It was to the apostle Paul. Notice what he wrote in **2 Corinthians 5:7-9**:

*⁷for we walk by faith, not by sight. ⁸ Yes, we are of good courage, and we would rather be away from the body and at home with the Lord. ⁹ So whether we are at home or away, **we make it our aim to please him.***

Paul says I (we) make it our aim, our goal, to please the Lord. Is there any other worthy goal in life than that? No, with a capital N.

Q. Is pleasing Christ your overriding goal in life? If not, why not?

Fifthly, *the flesh is in **direct opposition** with the Holy Spirit.*

Galatians 5:16-17 reminds us, *"But I say, walk by the Spirit, and you will not gratify the desires of the flesh. For the desires of the flesh are **against** the Spirit, and the desires of the Spirit are **against** the flesh, for these are **opposed** to each other, to keep you from doing the things you want to do."*

Look at the Amplified Bible's rendering, *"For the desires of the flesh are opposed to the [Holy] Spirit, and the [desires of the] Spirit are opposed to the flesh (godless human nature); for these are antagonistic to each other [continually withstanding and in conflict with each other], so that you are not free but are prevented from doing what you desire to do."*

It is important to know that the sinful flesh and the Holy Spirit are in no way agreeable with one another. Not only that be we read in this passage that they are mortal and real enemies and foes. They do not help each other or even accommodate one another. No, they are opposed in the greatest way possible and we cannot hope to bring pleasure to the heart of God and sit on the fence when it pertains to how we walk spiritually. The flesh and the Spirit are complete opposites. Our most fundamental choice as believers is choosing each day, each moment, which to obey.

Someone wrote, *"There is no such thing as peaceful coexistence between the **flesh** and the **Spirit**. Coexistence, yes. Peaceful coexistence, no. There can be no compromise between the flesh and the Spirit because to capitulate to sin is to violate the Spirit. If the flesh is up, the Spirit is down; if the Spirit is up, the flesh is down."*

Sixthly, *we must give no **authority** to the flesh in our lives.*

This is what **Romans 13:13-14** is saying, *"Let us behave decently, as in the daytime, not in orgies and drunkenness, not in sexual immorality and debauchery, not in dissension and jealousy. Rather, clothe yourselves with the Lord Jesus Christ, and do not think about how to gratify the desires of the sinful flesh."*

The apostle Peter writes, *"Dear friends, I urge you, as aliens and strangers in the world, to abstain from sinful desires, which war against your soul."* (**I Peter 2:11**)

The question is, what is the ***problem*** with the flesh in us?

Listen to what Paul says further to the Romans, *"So I find this law at work: When I want to do good, evil is right there with me. For in my inner being I delight in God's law..."*

*We need to know that the Spirit is willing and able, but the flesh is **weak** and **unredeemable**.*

Paul continues in Romans 7: *"but I see another law at work in the members of my body, waging war against the law of my mind and making me a prisoner of the law of sin at work within my members."*

*We need to remind ourselves that our flesh is a **magnate** to the law of sin.*

*We need to know and admit that in our flesh, we are **desperate people** in need of divine deliverance.*

As you can see, the sinful flesh we are saddled with until our eternal graduation is hopelessly helpless to give us any help in the spiritual realm.

What is Paul's conclusion to all of this. Look at verse 24 of Romans 7.

*"**What a wretched man I am**! Who will rescue me from this body of death? Thanks be to God—through Jesus Christ our Lord! So then, I myself in my mind am a slave to God's law, but in the sinful nature a slave to the law of sin."*

What is Paul saying by way of a conclusion to the flesh in our Christian lives?

Let the great prince of preachers, **Charles Haddon Spurgeon** sum it up for us. *"The worst enemy we have is the flesh. Augustine used to pray, "Lord, deliver me from that evil man, myself." All the fire that the devil can bring from hell could do us little harm if we did not have so much fuel in our nature. It is the powder in the magazine of the old man that is our perpetual danger. When we are guarding against foes without, we must not forget to be continually on our watchtower against the foe of foes within... You are pulled about by two contrary forces: You are dragged downward by the flesh, and you are drawn upward by the Spirit. They will never agree. These two* *powers are always contrary one to the other. If you think that you can help God by getting angry, you make a great mistake. You cannot fight God's battles with the devil's weapons. It is not possible that the power of the flesh should help the power of the Spirit."* **(Source: https://www.preceptaustin.org/galatians_517-18)**

THE HOLY SPIRIT.

In my humble opinion, **Romans 5-8** are the most important chapters in the Newer Testament concerning the Christian life and walk. Let me tell you why I believe this.

In **Romans 6**, Paul develops the idea of our spiritual identity as it relates to Christ's death and resurrection. He lets us know that God has not only freed us from *the penalty and guilt of sin* but more practically, He has freed us and is freeing us from *the very power of sin* that so easily seeks to master us. That truth is a fact. It is ***already*** an accomplished work for us. Notice that we do not grow into this or in time finally *"deserve"* it, but it is a ***free gift*** just as much as our initial salvation is. It is important that we *know, consider* and *receive these divine truths*. A lot of Christians *know*. Others *consider* it and hope it can be so in their life but too few *receive* it as fact and live it out with confidence and empowerment. That is my personal passion for all of God's children. I hope it is becoming ***yours*** as well as you read this book.

In **Romans 7**, Paul relates to the Roman Christians the power and potential domination of our own sinful flesh. Self or our flesh in its many forms seeks to control us from sunup to sundown. Paul says, what we want to do, we can't seem to regularly do. What we do not want to do, we find ourselves doing and even longing to do in increasing measure. It is a bad scene all the way around. Paul reminds the Romans that bad old "I" or self is what seeks to dominate their Christian life and walk. Yet all is not lost. There is a divine – *solution to this madness inside!* Paul says that Christ is the only One who provides real and lasting spiritual relief and victory over the world, the flesh and the devil. *"Wretched man that I am! Who will deliver me from this body of death?"*

Now if we stop at the end of chapter 7, we receive great hope and encouragement. *But, in God's wisdom, it is not the end of the story.* The story is just plain incomplete without **Romans 8** and the work of the Holy Spirit in our lives.

The Spirit in essence is the *exclamation point* to what Paul discusses in chapters 6 and 7. The Holy Spirit is the power and means to apply the truths of both chapters. He is the answer to sin, self and the cross and how we step into spiritual victory which by the way *- is applied effectively only through the Holy Spirit's working.* Without a proper understanding. Without an honest welcoming of the Holy Spirit into every aspect of our Christian life, we are left with more self, more flesh, more defeat and in the end, miserable disappointment. Unfortunately, that is how many of God's children are living today. That may be your story up to now. Yet, I remind you that it is not God's desire or best for His children – and that includes - **YOU**. It has come to be Satan's main course at his deplorable open-air restaurant, and we must move on from him.

The Holy Spirit's Work in The Christian Life

It has been a nearly a decade now that our family and hundreds of thousands of others in our area experienced some of the roughest, most devastating weather for this part of New Jersey in our lifetime. Many homes lost their power for at least three days and many for six or more. I was totally unaware and shocked how much devastation can come from a widespread *"power failure."* No electric. No water. No Internet. No relief from the ninety-degree plus temperature. It made me keenly aware of how little I am in control. Some homes were equipped with generators, but most did not have them. Those who used a generator were able to power certain parts of their home while the rest of the home was without. I got to thinking that - ***Generators seem to symbolize spiritually to me a form of the real thing but not entirely the real thing.***

And that is what we have today in most of our churches! Paul says we have a form of godliness but without the power. *(2 Tim.3:5)* A generator and the full power of electric are close in appearance but far reaching in comparison. Christendom these days seems to be plagued with plenty of form and little substance or sizzle. It seems to me that we are missing the most important part of the puzzle – ***real electric***! The ***Holy Spirit*** is the "real electric" and it is the very "dynamite of God", but if we are not plugged into His power grid, then we can claim little or nothing of His power and light.

One of the observations I have made in my thirty years as a follower of Christ is that many evangelicals are either afraid of the Holy Spirit, unaware of His place in their Christian life or plain deceived by the Enemy as to the desperate need they have for His place in their lives. His ministry toward His church is to *mature believers in their faith* so that they can be a shining light and witness to a lost world. His ministry toward every believer in Christ is to *fill them with His power* so that they can live and demonstrate the life of Christ within them. The Holy Spirit is God and because He's God, He is *power*. He is not responsible for *"barely Christian"* living or an anemic Christian living we see covering the Christian landscape these days. When the Holy Spirit is free to dominate the life of a Christian – there you will find divine authority and great spiritual influence. That has nothing to do with denominational flavor or religious belief or even what you say or believe about the Holy Spirit. It is all about His rightful and healthy influence in our lives.

The Spiritual Man or Woman

The spiritual man or woman has the Holy Spirit dwelling in him, filling him, leading him, teaching him, empowering him. Through the new birth, which is God's own life, eternal and uncreated, this has been imparted to him or her and now Jesus Christ is their very life. (Col. 3:4)

The spiritual man has a threefold relationship to the Lord Jesus Christ, which is manifested in his *character*, in his *conversation*, and in his *conduct*.

The spiritual man has **accepted** Christ as his - Savior.
The spiritual man has **yielded** to Christ as his - Lord.
The spiritual man has **appropriated** Christ as his Life.

Q. Is your Christian life mostly decided by the FLESH or the SPIRIT, and how do you know it?

Look what Paul has to say in 2 Corinthians 3 and verse 18.

"And all of us, as with unveiled face, [because we] continued to behold [in the Word of God] as in a mirror the glory of the Lord, are constantly being transfigured into His very own image in ever increasing splendor and from one degree of glory to another; [for this comes] from the Lord [Who is] the Spirit." (**Amplified Version**)

If we are connected right to the Holy Spirit's power, then we will be growing and changing as we behold (*cling to meditate on*) God's life changing Word! Let me ask you an important question. *Is it the Pastor's job to change you or is it the Holy Spirit's job?* Listen, a Pastor can plant precious seeds in your life and someone else can come along and water that seed, but it is God who causes all things to grow and change! (I Cor. 3:8) Satan does not want you to change because he knows that if you change, then others will eventually change around you.

Real, lasting change and spiritual growth comes from the Holy Spirit's work in our lives. It is an ***inside job*** not a cosmetic one. That is why we need His power daily, moment by moment. Without it, we are stuck on our own island, in our own strength and we are unapproachable even to the Holy Spirit. I love what Smith Wigglesworth writes about this.

"Do not be satisfied with anything less than the knowledge of a real change in your nature, the knowledge of the indwelling presence and power of the Holy Spirit. Do not be satisfied with a life that is not wholly swallowed up in God."

In summary, the old nature and the flesh just doesn't cut it when we realize that the Christian life is not natural but supernatural. This life is not from us, but from Christ. If we are to walk in consistent victory and freedom, we must trust the Holy Spirit to do in us and through us what He can only do.

Mark Bubeck, in his book, *The Adversary,* sums it up for us, *"The flesh is a built-in law of failure, making it impossible for the natural man to please or serve God. It is a compulsive inner force inherited from man's fall, which expresses itself in general and specific rebellion against God and His righteousness. The flesh can never be reformed or improved. The only hope for escape from the law of the flesh is its total execution and replacement by a new life in the Lord Jesus Christ."*

Beloved, there is a distinct difference between a Christian who is fleshly, and earth centered and minded and those who are filled to overflowing with the Spirit of God!

I like Dr. Tony Evans illustration, *"Imagine a `bucket is moved, the water spills out, drenching the objects surrounding it. When we are full of the Spirit, "living water" inevitably spills out in our singing mouths, our dancing feet and our clapping hands. Those around us are refreshed by the splash! For the Spirit-led believer in Christ, worshipping, like witnessing, is an automatic expression of who we are."*

Does this "picture" that Paul paints here resemble you and me? If not, why not?

Has there ever been a time when you asked God the Holy Spirit to fill you with Himself? To pour out and over you His mighty power to overflowing? If you haven't or you may believe that there a *"list of conditions"* to see His power in your life, you must think again. He has promised to give the Holy Spirit to them that ask Him. We need to forever realize that without a budding, growing relationship with the Holy Spirit, we are dead in the water as believers in Christ. ***Completely dead.*** While we might give a good show of living, God and Satan both know where we are in the scheme of things and sooner or later – it will all come out in the wash.

<u>10</u>

At the End of Our Days

"Do you think all Christians die happy? Not on your life! Some of them die as miserable sinners. Why? Because they've misused their time and wasted their lives. Many of you have laid dying on a hospital bed and prayed, "Lord, if you would only spare me, I'll do this, that, or the other." Well, have you done it?" -Leonard Ravenhill

John Kenneth Galbraith was a noted economist in the early 1900s who was called upon by many dignitaries to help sort the economic markets. He wrote the following story in his autobiography about his housekeeper:

"It had been a wearying day, and I asked Emily to hold all telephone calls while I had a nap. Shortly thereafter the phone rang. Lyndon Johnson was calling from the White House. 'Get me Ken Galbraith. This is Lyndon Johnson.' 'He is sleeping, Mr. President. He said not to disturb him.' 'Well, wake him up. I want to talk to him.' 'No, Mr. President. I work for him, not you.' When I called the President back, he could scarcely control his pleasure. 'Tell that woman I want her here in the White House."

Emily the housekeeper understood an important truth—she was a servant to one man and obeyed his wishes explicitly. Her loyalties were to Mr. Galbraith alone. What a great example of a true servant. *(Source: Reader's Digest, December 1981)*

One of these days, all of us who are saved are going to give account for our lives *after* we were saved. *After* is the key word. The Bible calls this accounting the "judgment or bema seat of God or Christ." Notice the words of Paul to the Roman believers,

"For we will all stand before the judgment seat of God; for it is written, "As I live, says the Lord, every knee shall bow to me, and every tongue shall confess to God." So, then each of us will give an account of himself to God." (14:10-12 ESV)

Then, Paul reminds the Corinthian church in his second letter the same thing when he writes,

"So, whether we are at home or away, we make it our aim to please him. For we must all appear before the judgment seat of Christ, so that each one may receive what is due for what he has done in the body, whether good or evil. Therefore, knowing the fear of the Lord, we persuade others." (2 Cor. 5:9-11)

There is a final test that we will take. It will not be a multiple-choice exam. It will not be a true or false test. It will be more like an essay – an essay of our life once we came to faith in Christ. We will not give an account for our **sins** because they were nailed to the cross. Our accounting will not be centered on our **sins against** Christ but our **service in** Christ. What were our deeds **motivated by** when we served Christ? Were we motivated by the pleasure of men or God?

Did our Christian works have "eternal substance" tied to them or were they characterized by works that were sown in the flesh? How did we faithfully navigate through the trials and disappointments of life? Did we "endure" or did we complain and become bitter and sour? This is the accounting that we must give when we stand before our Savior one day. Do not expect this subject to be talked about much in your church but it is every bit the word of God as John 3:16 and we all like that verse!

Question: *Should we not be a whole lot sober, on the border of being fearful because of knowing this?*

Paul says in 2 Corinthians 5:11 – *we should*. Not a fear that paralyzes us for the rest of time but a fear and a respect for the weight of such an upcoming meeting. Maintaining your freedom over sin, the flesh and the devil is easier when you know that your life will be evaluated one day by the One who eyes are like *fire.* (Rev. 1:14 - ESV)

Paul also reminds the Corinthian church about this final spiritual evaluation in his first letter with a little more detail.

"For no one can lay a foundation other than that which is laid, which is Jesus Christ. Now if anyone builds on the foundation with gold, silver, precious stones, wood, hay, straw each one's work will become manifest, for the Day will disclose it, because it will be revealed by fire, and the fire will test what sort of work each one has done. If the work that anyone has built on the foundation survives, he will receive a reward. If anyone's work is burned up, he will suffer loss, though he himself will be saved, but only as through fire." (ESV)

Notice the word *"fire"* or *"burned up"* is used four times in these few short verses. ***Fire*** in the scriptures (among other things) is a symbol of purity or holiness. One day we will not only stand to explain our Christian life to the One whose eyes are fire, but our works and our motives will be ***tested*** by "fire" and accessed for what they really were. We may think that we are getting away with our selfish and fleshly living ***here,*** but that kind of living will be revealed clearly ***there*** on that day! That alone should spur us to sober and responsible living. This sober truth can either be accepted and as a motivator or we can ignore it and minimize it to our own peril and disappointment. It is really that simple.

I am reminded of what the great statesman Daniel Webster was once asked, *"What is the greatest thought that can occupy a man's mind?* He replied: ***"My accountability to God".*** That it is. Jesus wants you to walk in freedom and in His identity the rest of your days. Yes, there will be some days when you bask in its warmth and other days when you desperately search for its importance. But with all that you do, make certain that you never forget the price that Jesus paid on the cross to buy your spiritual liberty. He paid a debt that He didn't owe; because we had a debt that we could never in a trillion years - satisfy.

An awesome poem written by the great 20th century spiritual giant, Leonard Ravenhill, captures for us what it means to ***choose*** to make a difference in this life and really for all eternity. Let this poem sink in before you charge on to the next chapter.

"It will not make much difference, friend, a hundred years from now, if you live in a stately mansion or on a river scow,

*If the clothes you wear are tailor-made or pieced together somehow, if you eat big steaks or beans or cake - **a hundred years from now.***

It won't matter your bank account or the make of car you drive, for the grave will claim the riches and fame and the things for which you strive.

There's a deadline that we all must meet, and no one will be late, it won't matter then all the places you've been, each one will keep the date.

We will only have in eternity – what we gave away on earth, when we go the grave, we can only save the things of eternal worth.

*What matters, friend, the earthly gain for which some men always bow? For your destiny will be sealed, you see – **a hundred years from now!"***

Eternity has no time for time. Time is just a warmup band for eternity.

What are you living for exactly these days? That is not just a cliché question but one that all of us must consistently answer lest we become a slave to the world, the flesh and the devil.

If you are in any way a horseracing enthusiast, you will certainly recall back in 1973 a racehorse named *Secretariat*, who became a legend in his own time. Not only did Secretariat win the Triple Crown of Thoroughbred Racing, but he did it with an unprecedented performance. At the Belmont Stakes, he not only won the race by 31 lengths, but he set new records along the way as he went faster with each phase of the run. For one-and-one-half miles, that famous thoroughbred ran faster every second. Secretariat was accelerating at such an incredible pace that his trainer noted if the race had been extended another lap, his heart would have literally exploded. It is always tempting to settle into status quo performance, but the greatest joy is found in straining ahead to not just finish, but to finish well (2 Timothy 4:7). ***(Source:"Retirement or Refirement", a sermon by Max Lucado)***

As we close this book and we move on with a sense of great responsibility and joy, let us be resolved to letting Christ, who is our life, have His full sway in our lives until we leave this poor, broken world for a new and glorious world where we be known as we are fully known. I encourage you to read this book on a yearly basis or at least every couple of years. I strongly implore you to share it with a few others as well. Be the one who suggests to your small group that you study and discuss the materials, both as a book and as a small group study. For the glory of God and the better understanding of the Christian life, to as many as possible across the globe, may it ever be.

In Christ, Your Co-laborer in ministry,

Chris J. Gregas

*Chris J. Gregas is a child of God and is passionate about teaching the people of God how to be more spiritually free than they have ever been. He is the husband of Janet for over 30 years, the father of four adult children and pop-pop to three grandchildren and one on the way. He is a teaching pastor, a hospice chaplain, an entrepreneur/leader with a technology company and an avid writer and speaker who regularly travels to South America to teach. You can promptly reach Chris @ **chasingdaylightstrategies @gmail.com** or on Facebook @ Christopher Gregas. He is available to lead a conference or speak at your venue as the Lord leads and in conjunction with time availability.*

Blessings. CJG

Other Books from Chris J. Gregas

- The Identity Driven Life: Why
- Knowing Who You Are Is Just as Important as Knowing Why You Are
- The Identity Driven Life - Small Group Study Guide
- The Identity Driven Life 2 – The Sequel
- The Identity Driven Life 2 – Small Group Study Guide
- Fearational: The Church in the Era of Covid-19
- The Healing Power of Gratitude
- 25 Days of Christmas Devotional
- A Blockbuster Trade: Trade Satan's Lies for God's Truth
- A Blockbuster Trade: Trade Satan's Lies for God's Truth - Small Group Study Guide
- Blessings All Day the Throne Room
- Surviving the Grind Without Becoming the Powder: 365 Daily from Meditations to Encourage and Challenge Entrepreneurs and Sales Leaders

Made in the USA
Columbia, SC
02 August 2024

39853562R00090